100%

Job Search Success

GWENN WILSON, MA

THIRD EDITION

CENGAGE
Learning·

Australia • Brazil • Japan • Korea • Mexico • Singapore • Spain • United Kingdom • United States

100% Job Search Success,
Third Edition
Gwenn Wilson

Product Director: Annie Todd

Senior Product Manager: Shani Fisher

Senior Content Developer: Judith Fifer

Associate Content Developer:
Danielle Warchol

Content Coordinator: Rebecca Donahue

Product Assistant: Kayla A Gagne

Media Developer: Amy Gibbons

Production Management, and Composition:
Manoj Kumar, MPS Limited

Production Manager: Elena Montillo

Senior Art Director: Pam Galbreath

Manufacturing Planner: Sandee Milewski

Rights Acquisition Specialist:
Shalice Shah-Caldwell

Marketing Brand Manager:
Jennifer Levanduski

Senior Marketing Manager: Lydia LeStar

Photo Researcher: PreMedia Global

Text Researcher: PreMedia Global

Interior and Cover Design: Suzanne Nelson,
essence of 7

Cover Image: © Elena Elisseeva/
Shuttestock.com (for front cover image)
© Luba V Nel/Shuttestock.com (for back
cover image)

Library of Congress Control Number: 2013948983

ISBN-13: 978-1-285-43005-8

ISBN-10: 1-285-43005-0

Cengage Learning
200 First Stamford Place, 4th Floor
Stamford, CT 06902
USA

Cengage Learning is a leading provider of customized learning solutions with office locations around the globe, including Singapore, the United Kingdom, Australia, Mexico, Brazil, and Japan. Locate your local office at: **www.cengage.com/global**

Cengage Learning products are represented in Canada by Nelson Education, Ltd.

To learn more about Cengage Learning Solutions, visit **www.cengage.com**

Purchase any of our products at your local college store or at our preferred online store **www.cengagebrain.com**

Printed in the United States of America
1 2 3 4 5 6 7 17 16 15 14 13

Table of Contents

4 RESUMÉ AND COVER LETTER DEVELOPMENT 75

© Istockphoto.com
/Yuri_Arcurs

PART 3   THE ART OF THE INTERVIEW / 147

 ## 7   SUCCESSFUL INTERVIEWING 149

SelectStock/the Agency Collection/getty images

8 AFTER THE INTERVIEW 177

Ariel Skelley/Getty Images

9 PROFESSIONALISM IN THE WORKPLACE 205

© Stephen Coburn
/Shutterstock.com

Preface

HOW WILL THIS TEXT HELP ME?

If you are reading this book, chances are that you are close to completing your college education and are preparing to seek employment in your field. Your dedication and perseverance are about to pay off as you embark on your career. Congratulations on reaching a significant milestone!

You are likely to find that there are many details involved in the job search process. Preparing your portfolio, revising your resumé, using networking and social networking tools, writing cover letters and other correspondence, and preparing a professional wardrobe are examples of the tasks you will need to complete in preparation for seeking employment. In addition to these tangible elements, you will need to know and practice appropriate interview etiquette, how to respond effectively to certain questions in the interview, and how to present yourself as confident, well prepared, and competent.

100% Job Search Success covers topics that are fundamental to successful job-seeking efforts. Following are the main themes from topics that are included in the text. Use these to get a general idea of the book and to see how each topic supports you in a successful job search.

- **KNOWING YOURSELF AND YOUR INDUSTRY:** Knowing your interests and abilities will help you find a good match between your professional goals and an employment situation. Understanding the requirements and standards of your field will allow you to carry out your responsibilities according to criteria for success in your profession.

- **ASSESSING AND DEVELOPING YOUR SKILLS:** There are certain skills such as leadership and understanding your strengths and weaknesses that contribute to your success in the job search. Developing these skills before you embark on your job search will work to your advantage.

- **LEARNING TO NETWORK AND ESTABLISH PROFESSIONAL RELATIONSHIPS:** A significant factor in the job search is establishing professional relationships. Learning to network skillfully will help you develop relationships and a place in the professional world.

▶ **CREATING AN EFFECTIVE RESUMÉ:** A resumé is effective when it influences a potential employer to invite you for an interview. Learning to create an effective resumé and complete other types of job-related correspondence will help you establish positive contact with employers.

▶ **DEVELOPING A PROFESSIONAL PORTFOLIO:** Showcasing your abilities to prospective employers is an important part of the job search. Appropriately selecting and displaying your most successful work will contribute to obtaining the job of your choice.

▶ **DEMONSTRATING PROFESSIONALISM:** Demonstrating professional etiquette—showing good manners—is also likely to make you stand out in the interviewer's mind. Paying attention to the etiquette of particular situations, such as mealtime interviews, is especially critical. The impression you make with your attire and grooming significantly impacts other aspects of the relationships you build during the job search. Learning to consider acceptable business dress when selecting a professional wardrobe will add to your professionalism.

▶ **DEVELOPING INTERVIEWING SKILLS:** After your first impression, the interview is where the interviewer learns more about you. Attention to the details of successful interviewing is more likely to make you stand out from other applicants and maximize your chances of getting the job.

▶ **NEGOTIATING AND DEALING WITH REJECTION:** Any job offer that you receive must be compatible with your goals and needs. The ability to negotiate effectively maximizes your chances of reaching an employment agreement that is mutually acceptable to you and the employer. Being rejected for a position during the job search is a natural part of the process. Feelings of disappointment are normal, but you can also use the rejection process to learn about yourself and your interviewing skills and to improve your job search skills.

▶ **WORKPLACE ISSUES:** Once you have that dream position you need to understand what it means to be a professional in the workplace and how to prepare yourself for entering (or re-entering) the workforce.

HOW TO USE THIS BOOK

100% Job Search Success is written to actively involve you in developing positive and productive job-seeking skills. The following features will help guide you through the material and provide opportunities for you to practice what you've learned:

▶ **BE IN THE KNOW:** A new feature to the third edition of *100% Job Search Success*, Be in the Know provides vignettes on real-world situations as they relate to the chapter content. The intent of this feature is to help students focus on the subject at hand, and how they can learn from the provided examples in these content areas.

▶ **LEARNING OBJECTIVES:** Learning objectives are provided as a guide to the information in each chapter. Use them to identify the important points of each chapter and to understand what you are supposed to learn. Learning objectives can also be used as a tool to measure what you have mastered and what you still need to work on. Remember that the learning objectives are a guide, and you are encouraged to expand on your knowledge according to your goals and interests.

▶ **CASE IN POINT:** In the middle of each chapter, a scenario ("Case in Point") illustrates an issue commonly faced by college students and that reflects the chapter contents. Use the questions following each scenario to stimulate your critical thinking and analytical skills. Discuss the questions with classmates. You are encouraged to think of your own ideas regarding how to apply concepts and to raise additional questions.

▶ **SELF-ASSESSMENT QUESTIONS:** Self-assessment questions ask you to reflect on and evaluate your personal development. These questions are intended to increase your self-awareness and ability to understand your decisions and actions. Self-assessment questions are also included on the companion web site so that you can print and respond to them and include them in your professional portfolio (discussed below).

▶ **CRITICAL THINKING QUESTIONS:** Critical thinking questions challenge you to examine ideas and to thoughtfully apply concepts presented in the text. Critical thinking questions encourage the development of thinking skills that are critical to efficient performance in school and in the workplace.

▶ **APPLY IT!** Following sections of the text, you will find activities that help you apply concepts discussed in the section to practical situations. Your instructor may assign these as part of the course requirements. If they are not formally assigned, you are encouraged to complete them for your own development. *100% Job Search Success* includes the following three types of activities, each indicated by its corresponding icon.

- **Individual activities** are directed at your personal development.

- **Group activities** typically include projects that are more successfully completed with the addition of several perspectives or broad research. A team effort adds to the success of these learning projects.

- **Internet activities** are intended to help you develop online skills. For example, you may research a topic or participate in an online discussion thread.

    You may find it helpful to combine the activity types. For example, an individual project may require Internet research. Some individual activities can be adapted to group activities, and vice versa. Use the activities as guides and modify them in ways that best support your learning. Activity sheets are available on the companion web site, and you are encouraged to print these and include them in your portfolio.

▶ **SUCCESS STEPS:** Success Steps are included throughout the text and provide concise steps for achieving various goals. Success Steps are offered as a summary of steps. Details of each step are discussed fully in the body of the text. Are you looking for success steps to achieve a specific goal? Use the table of contents by topic to locate the steps you need.

▶ **CHECK YOUR UNDERSTANDING:** Check Your Understanding, found on the companion web site, provides an opportunity for you to assess the effectiveness of your learning and to set goals to expand your knowledge in a given area.

▶ **SUGGESTED ITEMS FOR LEARNING PORTFOLIO:** A portfolio is a collection of the work that you have done. A *learning portfolio* is used to track your progress through school and a *professional portfolio* showcases your professional accomplishments. A *developmental portfolio* typically contains documents that illustrate your development over time. A professional portfolio contains finished projects and work that represents your best efforts and achievements and will be the emphasis of the portfolio you create as part of *100% Job Search Success.* Throughout *100% Job Search Success,* there are suggestions to include completed activities in your portfolio. Arranging your portfolio in a way that illustrates your professional development and showcases your best work will be useful for reviewing your progress and demonstrating your abilities.

As you read and complete the activities in *100% Job Search Success,* keep your long-term goals in mind and think about how you can apply these concepts to your everyday activities. Application is the key—and the more you practice, the more proficient you will become in using and communicating information.

Visit the companion web site for this textbook by going to **www.cengagebrain .com**, where you will find practice quizzes, flashcards, and additional resources to help support your success in college.

WHAT IS NEW IN THE THIRD EDITION?

The following changes have been made throughout the textbook:

▶ The text has been divided into three different parts to reflect common learning areas, and various chapters have been reordered within those parts.

• Part I: Preparing Yourself for the Job Search, contains the first two chapters from the previous edition: Chapter 1, Industry and Job Research, and Chapter 2, Assessing and Developing Skills for the Workplace.

- Part II: Tools for the Job Search, contains a new Chapter 3, Networking and Self-Promotion (formerly Chapter 4), Chapter 4, Resumé and Cover Letter Development (formerly Chapter 5), Chapter 5, Developing a Professional Portfolio (formerly Chapter 3), and Chapter 6, Professionalism in the Job Search, which is a combination of the former Chapter 6 and Chapter 9.

- Part III: The Art of the Interview, contains Chapter 7, Successful Interviewing, Chapter 8, After the Interview (which is a combination of the former Chapter 8 and Chapter 9), and a new Chapter 9, Professionalism in the Workplace.

▶ A new feature, Be in the Know, has been added to the beginning of each chapter.

▶ Cases in Point have been moved to the middle of each chapter and have been changed to encourage student participation and discussion.

The following list includes changes by chapter, to assist instructors in transitioning to the Third Edition of *100% Job Search Success*.

CHAPTER 1:

▶ The section "Professional Socialization" has been moved to Chapter 6, Professionalism in the Job Search.

CHAPTER 2:

▶ A new section "Identifying and Developing Soft Skills" focuses on how to discover the particular skills and highlight them to potential employers.

CHAPTER 3:

▶ The section "Using Social Networking in the Job Search" has been updated to include recent survey information about the job search process and the use of social media in the job search.

▶ A new section, "Personal Branding," has been added to define personal branding in the job search, and offers strategies for building a personal brand.

▶ The section "Other Networking Techniques" has been updated to include "The Informational Interview" (formerly in Chapter 7), and information about attending job fairs and using networking business cards as job search tools has been added.

CHAPTER 4:

▶ The section "Purpose of the Resumé" has been updated with more current information.

▶ The section "Other Types of Correspondence" has been expanded to include information about the purpose and use of various types of correspondence in the job search to include the application letter, the networking letter, the prospecting letter, and the career change letter.

CHAPTER 6:

▶ Chapter 6 was renamed "Professionalism in the Job Search."

▶ The section "Professional Socialization" was moved from Chapter 1 to Chapter 6.

▶ A new section "Video Chat Interview Etiquette" was added to address the increasing use of video chat to conduct interviews.

▶ The sections "First Impressions" and "Dressing for the Interview" were moved from the old Chapter 6. The section "Dressing for Success" was eliminated.

CHAPTER 7:

▶ A new section "Strategies for Successful Interviewing" was renamed from "Successful Interviewing Tactics" and includes information on interview logistics, successful interviewing techniques, dealing with feelings of nervousness, and the importance of nonverbal behaviors.

▶ A new section "Types of Interviews" was added to include information on traditional interviews, behavioral interviews, and situational interviews.

▶ A new section "Types of Interview Questions" provides information on and examples of common interview questions, behavioral interview questions, and situational interview questions. Information about illegal interview questions and questions to ask an employer during the interview were added to this section.

▶ The section "Questions to Ask an Employer During an Interview" was eliminated and the informational interview content was moved to Chapter 3.

▶ The section "Interview Follow-Up" was moved to Chapter 8.

CHAPTER 8:

▶ Chapter 8 was renamed "After the Interview."

▶ The section "Interview Follow-up" was moved from Chapter 7 to Chapter 8.

▶ A new section "Thank-You Notes" addresses the importance of sending either a handwritten or electronic thank-you note to the interviewer immediately following the interview.

▶ A new section "Negotiation" was moved from the old Chapter 8. It contains previously published material on the purpose of negotiation, assessing the organization, the dos and don'ts in negotiating, and accepting or declining a job offer.

▶ A new section "Dealing with Rejection" was added from materials previously published in the old Chapter 10.

▶ The sections "Self-Evaluation" and "Creating an Action Plan" from the old Chapter 10 were eliminated.

CHAPTER 9:

▶ Chapter 9 is a new chapter to this edition: "Professionalism in the Workplace."

▶ New sections in this chapter include:

- "Entering the Workforce," which speaks to changes recent graduates will find in their daily lives once entering the workplace.

- "Re-entering the Workforce," which gives direction to those who have been off the job market for a period of time.

- "Demonstrating Professionalism," which highlights the elements of professionalism that employers seek in their new employees.

- "Teamwork," which addresses the concept of teamwork in the workplace and the attributes which make up a valued and successful team player.

- "Mastering the Work-Life Balance," which talks about priorities in life and how to make some changes in one's life to achieve a balance between work life and personal life.

- "The Importance of Lifelong Learning," which addresses why lifelong learning is important and how it can help employees in their professional careers.

ANCILLARY MATERIALS

100% Job Search Success has a companion web site for students. Visit **www.cengagebrain.com** to access the web site. Available materials include practice quizzes, flashcards, and additional resources to help your students be successful in college.

An Instructor's Companion Site includes an Instructor's Manual, PowerPoint Slides, and a Test Bank. The instructor's resources can be accessed at **login.cengage.com**.

If you're looking for more ways to assess your students, Cengage Learning has additional resources to consider:

▶ College Success Factors Index 2.0

▶ Noel-Levitz College Student Inventory

▶ The *Myers-Briggs Type Indicator® (MBTI®) Instrument**

You can also package this textbook with the College Success Planner to assist students in making the best use of their time both on and off campus.

An additional service available with this textbook is support from TeamUP Faculty Program Consultants. For more than a decade, our consultants have helped faculty reach and engage first-year students by offering peer-to-peer consulting on curriculum and assessment, faculty training, and workshops. Consultants are available to help you establish or improve our student success program and provide training on the implementation of our textbooks and technology. To connect with your TeamUP Faculty Program Consultant, call 1-800-528-8323 or visit **www.cengage.com/teamup**.

For more in-depth information on any of these items, talk with your sales rep, or visit cengagebrain.com.

*MBTI and Myers-Briggs Type Indicator are registered trademarks of Consulting Psychologists Press, Inc.

part 1

Preparing Yourself for the Job Search

Part I of *100% Job Search Success* lays the groundwork for a successful job search.

Chapter 1: Industry and Job Research introduces how to use an understanding of your interests, abilities, and the requirements of your field or industry to establish and maintain your professional niche.

Chapter 2: Assessing and Developing Skills for the Workplace emphasizes the importance of recognizing your strengths and areas needing development and setting goals for professional development in preparation for the job search.

Industry and Job Research

LEARNING OBJECTIVES

By the end of this chapter, you will achieve the following objectives:

▶ Describe the personal characteristics and industry elements needed to secure a niche in an industry or field.

▶ Describe the elements of professional culture.

▶ Use suggested resources and techniques for researching industries and organizations.

▶ Use suggested resources and techniques for staying updated and current in an industry.

1

BE IN THE KNOW

Occupy My Time

The Bureau of Labor Statistics (BLS) is a valuable source of information for the job seeker, regardless of your age, education, economic situation, or career path.

One of the most helpful tools offered by the BLS is the *Occupational Outlook Handbook*. This publication, produced on a yearly basis, is the nation's premier source for career information. The profiles featured in the handbook cover hundreds of occupations and describe what workers in that occupation do, the work environment within the field, salary information, education requirements, and more. Each profile also includes BLS employment projections for the 2010–20 decade.

The following is a list of occupation groups researched by the BLS. Specific job titles are then listed under each category. Links provide detailed information about each job title within each group.

• Architecture and Engineering	• Legal
• Arts and Design	• Life, Physical, and Social Science
• Building and Grounds Cleaning	• Management
• Business and Financial	• Math
• Community and Social Service	• Media and Communication
• Computer and Information Technology	• Military
• Construction and Extraction	• Office and Administrative Support
• Education, Training, and Library	• Personal Care and Service
• Entertainment and Sports	• Production
• Farming, Fishing, and Forestry	• Protective Service
• Food Preparation and Serving	• Sales
• Healthcare	• Transportation and Material Moving
• Installation, Maintenance, and Repair	

Go to the Bureau of Labor Statistics web site at www.bls.gov/ooh to download the most current copy of the handbook. It is a valuable tool that you should keep in your job arsenal (source: Bureau of Labor Statistics).

UNDERSTANDING YOUR INDUSTRY AND YOUR PLACE WITHIN IT

In today's sluggish and uncertain economy, many people are returning to school to prepare for a new career, one that will support them now and into the future. The National Center for Education Statistics (NCES) projects that enrollment will rise by 11 percent for students under age 25

1

and 20 percent for students age 25 or older by 2020 (National Center for Education Statistics, 2012). Understanding your industry and its expectations will facilitate your transition to the workplace and support you in defining your professional role. Finding your place within your chosen profession is a process that takes into account your interests, education, professional goals, and abilities. It also includes an understanding, acceptance, and assimilation of professional requirements and values. Knowing the expectations of entry-level positions in your field is important and will contribute to your success as well as prevent disappointment.

YOUR INTERESTS

As you become familiar with more aspects of your profession, you will find certain elements more interesting than others. For example, a nursing student may find that she prefers pediatric nursing to critical care nursing. That student's interest contributes significantly to her establishing her place within the nursing profession. Keep a record of your interests and resources for pursuing them. Interests can—and should—change over time. You can expect to develop and refine your interests over the course of your career.

apply it

Interest Journal

GOAL: To identify your professional interests and establish resources that support their continued development

STEP 1: Create a hard copy or electronic journal. Select a format that is easily accessible to you, suited to your preferences, and one that you will use consistently.

STEP 2: Record and date your observations regarding the development of your professional interests as they become clear to you. Note significant influences and events that affect your interests. Set up periodic reminders to review your journal to see whether what was of professional interest to you is still valid and current.

STEP 3: Include activities such as interest inventories and other assessments that contribute to your insights about your interests. Your student services or career placement personnel are sources of these types of inventories. Record the contact information for mentors and professional colleagues who may be influential in helping you pursue your interests and goals.

STEP 4: Remember that the development of professional interests is a process that will continue during your academic preparation as well as throughout your career. Use this journal as a basis for your future professional growth and development.

YOUR ABILITIES

Specialized areas of a single profession provide a variety of opportunities for individuals with different skills and abilities. For example, an individual who has strong mathematical skills may choose to pursue a more quantitative path in her field than a person with strong verbal skills would. It is important to make an honest assessment of your skills and abilities and select the branch of your field where they will best be utilized.

YOUR VALUES

You are more likely to be happy in your work if the requirements of your position match your values. For example, if being with your family is a high priority, a position that requires travel five days a week may not be your best choice. Determine those values on which you can compromise and those on which you can't, and seek a position that is the best fit.

YOUR PERSONALITY

Personality traits such as assertiveness, patience, and risk-taking orientation as well as preferences for a certain type of work environment will influence the position you seek in your field. For example, if you are an extroverted individual who enjoys contact with and learning from other people, you will be most suited to (and probably happiest in) a position that offers those elements and related opportunities. Comfort zones can be stretched to a certain extent, but being in a situation that challenges your basic personality traits can interfere with your effectiveness on the job.

INDUSTRY REQUIREMENTS

Although you might have specific interests and excellent skills in a certain area, many fields have specific requirements for working in that area or performing certain tasks. These can range from specific experiences to certifications and continuing education units (CEUs). Some of these requirements, such as experience and certification, are summarized here. There may be others, depending on your field.

Experience

Some fields require specific experience as a requirement for a job. For example, some allied health fields require a specific amount of direct patient care experience before an individual may teach allied health students at the postsecondary level. Knowing the experience requirements of your industry that may affect your job research and pursuits will support you in seeking the experience you need to realize your long-term goals. Some entry-level positions may require experiences such as internships, part-time work, or involvement in a cooperative education setting.

Certifications

A wide variety of certifications are available in many fields. Some, such as nursing licenses, are required in order for an individual to practice. Others, such as certain technical certifications, may serve as an additional credential that enhances your marketability. Some organizations may require or prefer specific certifications. In some fields, having a minor course of study that complements your major is an asset. Familiarize yourself with the required and preferred certifications in your field. Your program chair or advisor should have this information available for you. Professional organizations in your field are likely to have the most current and up-to-date requirements. Be prepared to pursue additional certifications if requested by a potential employer or if it is a standard in your industry. Certifications can lead to increased salary, greater opportunity for advancement, and recognition in your field. In some cases, certifications may be required to meet safety and other standards.

Continuing Education

In a world where information and technology change on a constant basis, it is critical that your skills remain up to date. Continuing education, or courses taken after graduation while in the workplace, is one method by which professionals stay apprised of changes in their field and informed of current practices. Continuing education opportunities are available through professional organizations, local colleges, and professional publications. Continuing education requirements are frequently linked with maintaining current certification, which in turn may be required in order to practice in your field. Continuing education requirements vary according to the profession. Familiarize yourself with the specific requirements in your field.

1

apply it

Professional Requirements Research

Goal: To increase awareness of professional development resources and processes

STEP 1: Identify the professional organization(s) that defines certification and continuing education requirements for your field. Instructors and your program chair can assist you in finding this information.

STEP 2: Locate the organization's web site. Explore the site to find the requirements for certifications and continuing education. Include entry-level requirements such as minimum degree requirements and others such as internships. Make a note of the requirements.

STEP 3: In addition to the requirements, note resources such as publications, e-mail lists, and other tools that you can use to remain informed of continuing education and other professional development opportunities.

Personal Values

Personal values are those ideals that pertain to all fields and are appropriately used in all settings and most situations. Employers seek out these traits in a prospective employee and often write job descriptions to identify which of these skills the candidate possesses. It is wise to weave examples of these values into your cover letter and resumé, and during an interview.

Hansen and Hansen (n.d.) offer up the 10 most important personal values that employers seek, including these:

- **Honesty/Integrity/Morality.** The authors suggest that employers covet these values more than any others in the workplace.

- **Adaptability/Flexibility.** The ability to be both an independent worker and a team player, along with multitasking aptitude, are central to these values.

- **Dedication/Hard Work/Work Ethic/Tenacity.** This is your ability to problem-solve and stick with the task until the job is done.

- **Dependability/Reliability/Responsibility.** This work ethic should be no different from your discipline in school. Show up on time, prepared to work, and assume responsibility for your work.

▶ **Loyalty.** Employers expect you to be loyal to the company, even if the company is not reciprocating.

▶ **Positive Attitude/Motivation/Energy/Passion.** This may seem obvious. But showing drive, passion, and enthusiasm for your job will go a long way in getting you promoted.

▶ **Professionalism.** This goes without saying, but many workers get bogged down in company gossip and petty behavior. Rise above that line and stay there.

▶ **Self-Confidence.** If you are not confident in your abilities, how can your employer trust that you will get the job done? Strong self-confidence and self-esteem are highly regarded values in the workplace.

▶ **Self-Motivation/Ability to Work with Little or No Supervision.** "Teamwork" and "team player" remain corporate buzzwords, but your ability to stand on your own and make things happen is equally important.

▶ **Willingness to Learn.** Nothing is static in the business world. New technologies and products are always on the horizon. Be adaptable in your job to these changes and embrace them for your professional benefit.

SELF-ASSESSMENT QUESTIONS

- What other elements might be included in industry requirements for your field?
- What other personal values can you identify?
- How effective are your personal values? Which ones would you like to develop or improve?
- How can you determine the quality of your personal values?
- How can you develop your personal values? Where would you find resources?
- How can you acquire personal values while in college?

CASE IN POINT: GETTING CULTURED

Read the scenario below. Then, in groups or as a class, discuss the questions at the end.

Barbara Schenley is completing her final semester of her college program. She is beginning to consider employment possibilities. Barbara has maintained high grades and has been a successful student. As she prepares to leave the familiar surroundings of her school, Barbara has some concerns about finding her place in the professional world. She is concerned about finding a position that is right for her in an appropriate environment and is apprehensive about fitting in with her field's professional culture.

continued

1

continued

▶ What personal elements should Barbara consider in finding the "right" position?

▶ With which professional requirements does Barbara need to be familiar?

▶ What elements of professional culture should Barbara consider in her desire to fit in?

▶ What steps can Barbara take to develop her awareness of her field's professional culture?

▶ What resources can Barbara use to research her industry and specific organizations within it?

▶ Once Barbara is established in her field, how can she remain updated and informed?

PROFESSIONAL CULTURE

One of the definitions of *culture* provided by the Merriam-Webster Online Dictionary (2013) is "the set of shared attitudes, values, goals, and practices that characterize an institution or organization."* This also defines *corporate culture*, the tone or feeling that is predominant in an organization or company. Corporate culture is a product of expectations, standards, the quality of interpersonal relationships, and general atmosphere. Culture ultimately influences the effectiveness and efficiency of the organization. As an example, think about an organization or workplace you were in that felt positive and productive. Compare and contrast this image with a company or organization where the atmosphere was negative and perhaps even demoralizing. A corporate culture that nurtures a positive environment is typically productive and profitable. The following elements contribute to the culture of a profession or organization.

Dress Standards

Every profession has its own standards for appropriate dress. Within each field, dress standards may vary according to position. Dress

*By permission. From *Merriam-Webster's Collegiate Dictionary*®, 11th Edition © 2010 by Merriam-Webster, Incorporated (www.Merriam-Webster.com).

contributes to culture by defining the impression an employee's appearance conveys. In some fields, casual dress contributes to an easy-going and informal environment. In others, more business-like attire, such as suits, creates a more formal atmosphere. Of course, dress is not the only element that constitutes culture, but it is a significant component. Remember that how you dress will determine in part how you are accepted into your professional or organizational culture. Learn and follow your organization's dress requirements. When attending a professional meeting or conference of professionals in your field, research dress expectations prior to attending.

Interpersonal Relationships

Deal and Kennedy (2000, p. 98) describe the *cultural network* as an informal, yet powerful, communication system that exists within an organization. The relationships and unofficial, casual communication within a profession or organization can significantly influence morale and attitude. It is important to be aware of the influence of informal communication and to use the cultural network in a constructive manner. For example, the informal network can be used to promote supportive and collaborative relationships or, conversely, to pass gossip that can be disruptive and harmful. Your thoughtfulness and judgment in participating in the cultural network can have a significant impact on how you are viewed by your colleagues and accepted into your professional and organizational culture.

Relationships in the workplace are affected by the way you communicate with others. Gain respect from and establish trust with your colleagues by avoiding gossip, rumors, and other questionable interactions. Communication that is honest, yet tactful, and based on verifiable information is most likely to contribute to effective and productive workplace relationships. Be approachable and open while maintaining a professional demeanor.

Communication Practices

For our purposes, *communication practices* will refer to more formal expression within a profession or organization. The chain of command, processes for making requests and suggestions, and protocols for conflict resolution are examples of formal communication practices. Organizations and professions typically have published policies and procedures for these types of communications. Examples include

Your manner of communicating and participating in the informal corporate culture can have a significant impact on how you are viewed by your colleagues.

1

the policy governing e-mail use in the workplace and a standard format for submitting a weekly report. Your awareness of these practices and your ability to use them effectively will also influence your success in finding your niche within the field or in an organization and fitting in with its culture. Following communication protocol is important to establishing effective working relationships.

Professional Authority

Each profession recognizes knowledgeable individuals and credible sources of expert information and advice in the field. Examples of professional authorities might be your professional organization, individuals recognized as experts in your field, or your supervisor. Likewise, organizations also have their lines of authority, which are referred to as the chain of command. Knowing your sources of professional information and expertise and using them appropriately to validate your activities and contributions will add to your credibility as you find your place within your field. Develop the ability to disagree respectfully and to substantiate your perspective with reliable data. For example, if you believe a deadline for a project is unrealistic, address the issue with your supervisor (or the appropriate individual), and substantiate your request for additional time with evidence of other assignments that you are in the process of completing.

Professional Values and Ethics

Values are those elements that an individual or organization holds as important. Examples of values include altruism, loyalty, peace, integrity, and wisdom (Ethics Resource Center, 2009). Values are the basis of an individual's or organization's vision. When group members share values, they provide a powerful foundation for prioritizing activities, making decisions, and formulating action (Industrial College of the Armed Forces, 1999).

Ethics are the embodiment of certain values and define ways in which individuals carry out values as reflected in daily activities. It is likely that your field will have its own set of values and a professional code of ethics that is based on universal principles. A professional code of ethics is the translation of principles that guide behavior and is intended to guide professional decisions and actions.

? **CRITICAL THINKING QUESTIONS**

▶ What ethical issues can you identify in current events?
▶ How does the consideration of ethics influence the decisions made about these events and their outcomes?

1

 apply it

Values and Ethics in Practice

GOAL: To translate professional values, ethics, and standards into action

STEP 1: Form a group of students interested in exploring professional values and ethics and how they are incorporated into daily practice in your field.

STEP 2: Ask each group member to obtain a copy of your profession's code of ethics, standards of practice, values statements, or other documentation of these aspects of your profession. These can be found online, or you may ask a faculty member or librarian for assistance in locating a copy. Consider using general business ethics if you have significant difficulty locating a field-specific code of ethics.

STEP 3: Ask group members to write their thoughts on how the values, ethics, and standards of your field are demonstrated in daily professional activities. One way to think about this is to ask yourself what actions demonstrate these values and how these actions can be incorporated into the tasks of your field.

STEP 4: Meet as a group and share your ideas. Combine them into a group statement of guidelines for actions and behaviors that reflect professional values and ethics.

STEP 5: To obtain feedback, share your final project with a faculty member or other professional from your field.

Professional values may differ from the personal values that you hold individually. Professional values reflect universal, socially responsible principles such as respect, responsibility, and integrity and are the concepts upon which ethics is based. Personal values are those values that reflect your individual belief system. Conflict between personal and professional values must be resolved by referring to your profession's values and its code of ethics. Decisions should be based on these values and on the code, with the interest of your clients in mind. Understanding your profession's code of ethics and being able to apply it to your daily practice is one method of establishing your professional integrity.

Self-Assessment Question

- What values would you identify as most important to an organization? Why did you choose these values?

SOURCES FOR INDUSTRY RESEARCH

There are a variety of resources available to you for researching your industry or profession. Many of these resources can also be used for researching individual companies. Resources are available on your campus, in your local community, and on the Internet, from national

1

and international sources. Information that will be helpful to you in researching a specific company includes a contact person, company history, recognition the company has received, and current projects and goals. Knowing the company's values and mission is also important. Consider the following suggestions for researching your field and specific companies.

THE INTERNET

The Internet provides a vast array of resources for researching various industries and companies. Hiring statistics, salary ranges, and other information can be accessed on the Web. If you know the URL of a specific site that provides the information you need, access the site directly. If you don't have a specific URL, conducting a search using key words can provide a significant amount of information. The following are suggested search terms for researching various aspects of your industry:

▶ Industry research

▶ Bureau of Labor Statistics

▶ Salary surveys

▶ Hiring statistics

▶ Your profession (for example, "physical therapy" or "computer programming")

If you are seeking information about a specific geographic location, conduct a search using the name of the city or town of interest. Look for the Chamber of Commerce web site or the official web site of the city or town. These web sites often have employment information for the area. Be aware of other sites that might offer useful information.

Individual companies can be researched in similar fashion using the Internet. Conduct a search using "researching individual companies" as your search term. Look for companies such as Hoover's (www.hoovers.com) that provide information about organizations in a variety of industries.

One way to stay abreast of current developments in your field is to subscribe to RSS (Real Simple Syndication) feeds that deliver current information and articles to your inbox. Instead of having to search for current information, it comes to you. To learn more about RSS feeds, research your professional organizations and other reputable groups in your field and explore their options for RSS feed

Internet research can provide you with important information about your field and organizations in which you have an interest.

subscriptions. Other options include electronic mailing lists, newsletters, and professional groups on social networking sites. In all cases, ensure that the information source is reputable and reliable.

GOVERNMENT SOURCES

The federal and state governments often have information related to hiring trends, projections for demand in various fields, and salary information. The Bureau of Labor Statistics (www.bls.gov) is the federal department that provides this type of information.

PROFESSIONAL ORGANIZATIONS

A professional organization is composed of individuals within a certain profession or trade. Professional organizations are typically formed at the international, national, and state levels. These organizations will usually have information specific to your field, including technical updates, changes in certification requirements, and legislative updates on issues relevant to the profession. If you are not currently familiar with your field's professional organization, faculty in your department may be able to provide you with the organization's name and contact information. Because professional organizations are more focused on your field than are general web sites and government sources, the

1

organization usually provides more specific and accurate information about your field and the specialty areas within it. For example, an automotive trade journal will be able to speak in depth about various specialties and techniques related to engine repair and maintenance. The information can be expected to be accurate and reliable.

NETWORKING

Networking refers to making contacts with individuals from whom you can learn about your profession in general or about specific opportunities within your field or locale. Formal networking can be accomplished at live events as well as virtually through social networking sites. Although you may meet networking contacts in informal situations, effective networking requires more than an informal approach. Careful planning and organization add to the effectiveness of your networking efforts. Both traditional and social networking are discussed in detail in Chapter 3.

Networking is often an effective method of researching employers, as many positions are not advertised. For example, employment needs are often communicated by word of mouth in professional circles. Being visible increases your access to these types of situations. Also, networking is often a more comfortable environment, as the formality and pressure of a formal interview are absent.

INFORMATIONAL INTERVIEWS

Informational interviews are formal appointments in which you interview a professional to obtain specific information regarding your field or the organization as part of your research efforts. As with networking, you will need to be prepared and organized by obtaining appropriate background information, having specific goals for the interview, and formulating relevant questions. To learn more about conducting informational interviews, use an Internet search tool with "informational interviews" as your search term. Informational interviews are covered in greater depth in Chapter 3.

Keith Brofsky/Getty Images

Relationships built through the networking process can provide you with information to develop your professional knowledge and contacts.

FACULTY

As instructors, your faculty members are well informed of current news and techniques in your field. They are familiar with local and

1

national professional organizations as well as local facilities and businesses that hire in your field. Consider exploring options with your faculty members. Inform them in advance of the information you are seeking, and set an appointment time so that both of you are prepared for the meeting.

CAREER SERVICES

Most schools have a department devoted to assisting new graduates in exploring and locating employment opportunities. Career placement personnel are knowledgeable about current hiring trends, practices, and opportunities, both locally and in other areas, and are also familiar with specific organizations. In addition to resumé writing, interviewing skills, and career interest assessments, career services personnel may be able to assist you with organizational research. Consider setting an appointment with a career services representative at your school. Don't wait until you are a graduating senior to take advantage of the benefits of career services. Visit career placement personnel during your first semester so you can apply their advice while you are in school.

PROFESSIONAL JOB COUNSELORS

There are numerous off-campus services that offer professional job and career counseling. Many do in-depth assessments of your interests, aptitudes, and personality factors that can influence your career planning. They may also provide coaching in writing resumés, setting up informational and hiring interviews, and completing other aspects of industry and job research. Keep in mind that these services can be costly. Professional job counselors can be found in your city's telephone directory or on the Internet. If you choose to use a specific counselor or service, be sure to research its history of service and to obtain references.

LIBRARIES

Reference librarians in your school or at the public library are familiar with numerous resources. Consult with reference librarians for assistance in researching areas of interest within your field.

1

apply it

Sources for Industry Research

GOAL: To establish a method and resources for conducting industry research

STEP 1: Select a method for recording and collecting resources you find during this activity. Be creative in selecting a method or combination of methods that is easily accessible and that you will use. For example, you may wish to establish an electronic folder in which you bookmark important web sites, but you may devise a paper filing system for the business cards of professional contacts.

STEP 2: Record and/or file contact information for professional organizations, government sites, professional contacts, and other sources. Remember to select an organizational system that works for the materials you are organizing.

STEP 3: Keep your files updated as you receive new information and add new contacts.

STAYING CURRENT AND UPDATED

In today's information age, all professions grow and change at a rapid pace. In order to remain up to date in your field, it is essential that you have access to current information regarding technical skills, ethical and legal issues, and other elements that contribute to professional culture.

The same resources that provided information on industry and organizational research can also be used for obtaining updated information, provided the source is current. In addition to these resources, there are others that you can employ that will automatically provide you with current information. Consider the following resources for the remaining current in your field.

PROFESSIONAL ORGANIZATIONS

Professional organizations exist for the benefit of their professional members. Commitments that professional organizations make to their membership include providing continuing education opportunities, communicating technical developments in the field, and serving other general interests of constituents. Membership in your field's professional organization will typically provide you with access to new information and revisions to existing information, allowing you to remain current in your field. For example, members of a professional organization are typically informed of technical advances and political issues affecting their field. Professional organizations focus on collecting information and disseminating it to their members.

PROFESSIONAL PUBLICATIONS

Professional organizations usually publish an official journal or newsletter that informs readers of developments and research relevant to the field. In addition to publications from your professional organization, there are numerous journals and other materials from related fields that provide a broader perspective on your industry. As you progress in your professional development, you may become aware of related publications that will support your interests and goals. For example, teachers may find journals on child development a helpful supplement to professional teaching publications.

Keep a record of information from professional journals and seminars to develop your knowledge of your field.

CONTINUING EDUCATION AND CONFERENCES

One of the benefits of being a member of a professional organization is that you will also receive information about workshops, seminars, and other continuing education opportunities. Some fields require a specific amount of documented continuing education. In other cases, professionals pursue formal learning events to expand their knowledge and interests or to explore new areas. Professional conferences, frequently sponsored by professional organizations, are excellent sources of learning, as numerous choices of events in one place offer a variety of learning opportunities for one registration fee. Professional conferences also provide excellent networking opportunities.

Continuing education may be a requirement of your field.

CERTIFICATION AND LICENSURE BOARDS

Fields that require a license or certification to practice will typically have a credentialing organization that administers certification activities. Licensure requirements vary from state to state and are monitored by the individual states. Certification organizations and state licensure boards typically communicate updates of policies, requirements, and regulations to individuals holding credentials. Organizations and state boards also have web sites and contact information; contact them with any questions or concerns regarding professional credentials.

Some fields require a person to undergo a criminal background check prior to becoming certified. The certification board in your field can provide information regarding whether criminal background checks are a routine practice. It is important to be aware that what you do now can affect your opportunities in your field. For example, drug use or other forms of illegal behavior on your record can prevent you from obtaining the position of your choice.

ELECTRONIC COMMUNICATION

Electronic communication enables nearly immediate and efficient communication via e-mail, electronic mailing lists, RSS feeds, professional online social networking groups such as LinkedIn, and Web forums. Many professional organizations use e-mail to communicate with members. For example, an organization might send weekly e-mails summarizing events of the week. Web-based forums allow members to post questions and to share ideas related to their field. Electronic mailing lists such as Listserv or Yahoo! Groups allow information to be posted to a designated group as well as the opportunity to post resources (with regard for copyright, of course) and share information. These services typically require a subscription and may be free or available for a fee. Check with your professional organization for electronic communication tools that the organization might offer.

apply it

Program Resources

GOAL: To establish a community resource for industry research

STEP 1: Assemble a group of students from your program. Participants should be interested in developing a community resource that will support other students in researching your field.

STEP 2: Research and collect industry resources as described in the previous activity, Sources for Industry Research.

STEP 3: Assemble the resources into a format that can be easily accessed by students. Suggestions include a bulletin board or a notebook within your department. Or consider an online group using one of the professional social networking sites or a resource such as Yahoo! Groups. Your school librarian or learning resource center staff may also have suggestions for your particular school.

CHAPTER SUMMARY

As you begin your career, you will find many opportunities for professional growth and development. This chapter focused on how you can use an understanding of your interests, abilities, and the requirements of your field or industry to establish and maintain your professional niche. The elements of professional culture were explored as a way of understanding and becoming involved with the processes particular to your field. You also received suggestions for tools, such as professional organization and continuing education options, to research your field and further your professional development and to become socialized into your field.

POINTS TO KEEP IN MIND

In this chapter, several main points were discussed in detail:

- Finding your place within your chosen profession will be a process that takes into account your interests, professional goals, abilities, and an understanding and assimilation of professional requirements and values.

- Several personal and field-specific elements will influence how you determine your place in your field. These include your interests, abilities, experience, personal values, and certification and continuing education requirements.

- Finding your place in your field includes understanding your profession's culture. Elements of professional culture include dress standards, the way interpersonal relationships are conducted, communication practices, sources of professional authority, and professional values and ethics.

- Resources for researching your industry and specific companies include the Internet, government sources, professional organizations, networking activities, informational interviews, faculty members, career services, and professional job counselors.

- Resources for remaining current in your field include professional organizations, professional publications, continuing education and conferences, certification and licensure boards, and electronic communication tools.

1

CHECK YOUR UNDERSTANDING

Visit www.cengagebrain.com to see how well you have mastered the material in Chapter 1.

SUGGESTED ITEMS FOR LEARNING PORTFOLIO

Refer to the Developing Portfolios section at the front of this textbook for more information on learning portfolios.

- ▶ Reflection and Critical Thinking Questions: Include your written responses to these questions. Use them to review your development over time.

- ▶ Interest Journal: This activity will assist you in identifying your professional interests and resources for their pursuit. Keep this information to guide you in your career search and for future professional development.

- ▶ Professional Requirements Research: Develop a bank of professional development resources. Keep this information to guide you in your career search and for future professional development.

- ▶ Values and Ethics in Practice: The purpose of this activity is to assist you in applying concepts such as professional values, ethics, and standards to daily activities.

- ▶ Sources for Industry Research: This activity will support you in developing methods and resources for researching your industry in preparation for the job search.

- ▶ Program Resources: Work with peers to create a professional resource that benefits all of you. In your portfolio, note the process and resources that you use to complete this activity. Conducting a project such as this could be included on your resumé as a transferable skill.

REFERENCES

Deal, T. E., & Kennedy, A. A. (2000). *Corporate cultures: The rites and rituals of corporate life*. New York, New York: Basic Books.

Ethics Resource Center. (2009). Definitions of values. Retrieved February 21, 2013, from http://www.ethics.org/resource/definitions-values

Hansen, R. S., & Hansen, K. (n.d.). What do employers *really* want? Top skills and values employers seek from job-seekers. Retrieved February 21, 2013, from http://www.quintcareers.com/job_skills_values.html

Industrial College of the Armed Forces. (Ed.). (1999, Feb.). Values and ethics [Electronic version]. In *Strategic leadership and decision making* (Part 4, Chapter 15). National Defense University, Institute for National Strategic Studies. Retrieved February 21, 2013, from http://www.au.af.mil/au/awc/awcgate/ndu/strat-ldr-dm/pt4ch15.html

Merriam-Webster Online Dictionary. (2010). Culture. Retrieved February 21, 2013, from http://www.merriam-webster.com/dictionary/culture

National Center for Education Statistics. (2012). Fast Facts: Do you have information on college enrollment? Retrieved February 21, 2013, from http://nces.ed.gov/fastfacts/display.asp?id=98

CHAPTER OUTLINE

Buero Monaco/StockImage/Getty Images

Assessing and Developing Skills for the Workplace

LEARNING OBJECTIVES

By the end of this chapter, you will achieve the following objectives:

▶ Define technical skills, soft skills, and transferable skills.

▶ Define internship.

▶ Explain the importance that goals can have on success.

▶ Discuss goals that can be established while in school.

▶ Describe the different types of self-assessment tools.

▶ Discuss the various types of career-building activities that students can utilize to gain experience in their profession.

▶ Explain the purpose and goals of an internship.

▶ Discuss various methods one can use to locate an internship.

▶ Discuss tips on being successful in an internship.

▶ Demonstrate the ability to research possible internship sites.

2

BE IN THE KNOW

The Internship: Supervised Practical Training

As you will learn in this chapter, an internship is an excellent way to get experience in your field of choice. Not only will you receive college credit, you will be getting marketable skills that will transfer well when you enter the workforce.

This chapter gives several suggestions as to how to go about locating the best internship for your situation. Among those suggestions is to check internship web sites. One such site that may grab your attention is www.internships.com.

Internships.com maintains a student section where you will have access to the following information.

- **Database of internships.** This site lists thousands of internship positions from thousands of companies in all 50 states for fall, winter, spring, and summer opportunities.

- **The Internship Predictor®.** The Internship Predictor® is an assessment tool that gauges preferences in personality traits, interests, and values. This feature is quick and easy to use and may provide additional insight into which internship is best suited for your needs, interests, and abilities.

- **Internship Seeker 2.0.** This is a free download to your iPhone that provides mobile access to internship listings. Here you can save and manage your searches.

- **Student Resources.** This robust section offers students a wealth of information, including answering basic internship questions, guides to searching and applying for internships, interview strategies and tips, and more.

- **Eye of the Intern®.** This is a blog that is specific to internships. Blog updates are available via RSS feeds.

- **Internships Widget.** These are portable widgets that you customize and place on a blog, social network site, or your own web site.

When considering an internship, be sure to use all the resources available to you. Internships.com may be a good place to start.

SETTING GOALS FOR YOUR PROFESSIONAL PURSUIT

It is important to begin planning and preparing for your professional career while still in school. Being successful and competitive in your profession requires having well-defined goals. In addition to developing your skills and graduating, there are other goals that are important for students to achieve while attending college. These goals should be developed with an appreciation of the influence that both academic and extracurricular experiences can have on overall professional success. Actions that can contribute to goal achievement include the following (Bruce, n.d.):

▶ **Make a good impression while in school.** Faculty members, advisors, and other students may be the individuals who recommend you for a job.

▶ **Take leadership roles in and outside of school.** Develop and demonstrate your abilities to work with a variety of individuals. For example, being involved in school activities, community activities, or volunteer work demonstrates leadership and the ability to work with diverse individuals. If you are working in addition to attending school, taking leadership roles on the job also demonstrates this skill.

▶ **Find a mentor who can help guide and promote you and your professional pursuits.** A mentor is an individual who will guide and challenge you to develop both professional and personal skills. This individual may be a faculty member, graduate, or industry professional.

▶ **Be clear on your career objectives.** Develop an awareness of your professional direction and goals. Chapter 1 explored methods for establishing your niche in your profession. Develop career objectives based on where you want to be in your career.

▶ **Understand your strengths and weaknesses.** Explore how your strengths can contribute to your professional growth. Set goals for improving weaker areas. Use feedback from instructors, mentors, academic advisors, and employers to gain insight into your abilities and to set professional goals.

▶ **Gain professional experience while in school.** Participate in volunteer opportunities, co-op work, or an internship to gain experience in your field. Establish and demonstrate a strong work ethic during these opportunities.

SELF-ASSESSMENT QUESTION

- What goals do you need to establish that would help in your academic and professional success?

? CRITICAL THINKING QUESTION

▶ What is your reaction to the following statement? "Goals are important, but because goals change so much, writing them down is unnecessary." Provide a rationale for your response.

success steps for goal achievement

- Make a good impression while in school.
- Take leadership roles in and outside of school.
- Find a mentor who can help guide and promote you and your professional pursuits.

continued

2

continued

- Be clear on your career objectives.
- Understand your strengths and weaknesses.
- Gain professional experience while in school.

KNOW YOURSELF

Knowing your unique and individual traits will help you to market yourself effectively.

Digital Vision/Getty Images

Identifying and being aware of your existing knowledge, skills, experiences, and character traits is a necessary step toward being able to market yourself successfully. In school, students have the opportunity to use instructors' feedback to develop an understanding of their strengths and weaknesses in both technical and transferable skill areas.

Technical skills are generally thought of as those skills that are necessary to perform specific job tasks. You have likely learned specific technical skills during your studies and will learn more while on the job. *Transferable skills* are those abilities that can be easily transferred to a variety of work settings. But how does one acquire transferable skills?

IDENTIFYING AND DEVELOPING TRANSFERABLE SKILLS

You have recently graduated from your field of study, had a stellar academic career, and are ready to hit the job market. But wait—you've never held down a "real" job before. So how do you convince a prospective employer that you possess much more than a resumé and a diploma?

The secret is the identification and leveraging of your transferable skills. "One of the most important concepts you will ever encounter in the job-hunting process is that of transferable job skills," writes Katharine Hansen, Ph.D. (K. Hansen, n.d.). Transferable skills can come from any facet of life—classes, projects, sports, volunteer work, almost anything—that can follow you from your current situation and will be applicable to your new situation.

Dr. Hansen identifies five broad categories of transferable skills, including these:

▶ Communication. Skills in this area include the following:

- Speaking effectively
- Writing concisely

- Expressing ideas
- Providing appropriate feedback

▶ Research and planning. These include the following:
- Identifying problems
- Identifying resources
- Gathering information
- Solving problems

▶ Human Relations. Skills in this category consist of the following:
- Listening
- Motivating
- Cooperating
- Asserting

▶ Organization, Management, and Leadership: Skills in this area include these:
- Managing conflict
- Handling details
- Coordinating tasks
- Promoting change

▶ Work Survival. Skills in this category consist of the following:
- Managing time
- Meeting goals
- Organizing
- Setting and meeting deadlines

Dr. Hansen suggests that transferable skills should be the cornerstone of your cover letter, resumé, and interview methodology. Think in terms of all the skills that you have acquired through your experiences and how you can bring them to your new position. And be sure to articulate your skill set at every opportunity. It will pay off in your job search in the end.

IDENTIFYING AND DEVELOPING SOFT SKILLS

In concert with the transferable skills that you bring to the job search are your *soft skills*. Soft skills can be defined as your personal behaviors and traits that you demonstrate both in your personal and professional life. Some examples of soft skills include self-awareness, adaptability, critical thinking, problem solving, leadership, teamwork, communicating, likeability, risk taking, and time management (P. Klaus, n.d.).

Diversity Awareness

In the workplace, soft skills can also include diversity awareness. Diversity awareness is the demonstration of respect for individuals with disabilities and from different cultural groups, lifestyles, age groups, socioeconomic groups, and genders. It includes being aware of words and actions that may be offensive to others and refraining from using offensive elements in communication and other activities. Diversity awareness has expanded to include such aspects of diversity as various learning styles and learning differences as well as ways of thinking. The "smallness" of the world in the 21st century requires an open mind and willingness to learn from and about a variety of sources.

SELF-ASSESSMENT TOOLS

Conducting a self-assessment can be both challenging and rewarding. Various assessment tools help students to match their interests, skills, and personality type with their school and career goals. Depending on the outcome of the various self-assessment tests, individuals may at times find the need to reevaluate professional goals. Becoming more self-aware may prompt some students to consider other professions that better fit with their strengths, abilities, and personality type. If this is a consideration, students should seek out further guidance from individuals trained in career counseling.

A variety of self-assessment tools are available, often found online. The student services or academic advising department on your campus may also be able to provide resources for these tools. Assessment tools can include the following (University of California, Berkeley—Career Center, n.d.):

▶ **Interest inventories.** Interest inventories include the Strong Interest Inventory, the Self-Directed Search (SDS), the Campbell Interest and Skill Survey (CISS), and the Career Key (Dikel, 2002). The Strong Interest Inventory assesses your interests and matches them to careers. The inventory tells you where you might enjoy working, based on the interests you have in common with other individuals in a given profession. The Strong Interest Inventory does not measure ability or aptitude.

apply it

Self-Assessment Activity

GOAL: *To develop a clearer appreciation for and understanding of your strengths and weaknesses*

STEP 1: From the various self-assessment tools mentioned in this chapter, select one.

STEP 2: Conduct further research regarding this tool and take the test.

STEP 3: Write a brief report regarding your findings and what you discovered about yourself.

STEP 4: Consider placing your self-assessment test in your Learning Portfolio.

▶ **Personality tests.** Myers-Briggs Type Indicator (MBTI), Keirsey Temperament Sorter, and TypeFocus are examples of available personality assessment tests. These tests can provide information on how you communicate, gather information, and make decisions. They can also help you determine whether your personality fits the job that you are considering (Dikel, 2002). TypeFocus helps answer questions such as these: What are my personal strengths? What careers will I find satisfying? How do I use my strengths in a successful job search?

▶ **Skills inventories.** The Skills and Attributes Inventory (SAI) and the SkillScan assessment can help in defining your skills and abilities. SkillScan helps you identify your skills and how they apply to various careers. In addition, it provides the opportunity to identify careers in which your skills are most applicable. The tool also assists you in strategizing to develop your career and in writing your resumé to support your goals.

SELF-ASSESSMENT QUESTION

• What self-assessment tool interests you the most and why?

CRITICAL THINKING QUESTION

▶ What is your reaction to the following statement? "Other than the fact that self-assessment tests are fun to take, there is no validity to them and they are a waste of time." Provide a rationale for your response.

GAINING EXPERIENCE: THE OVERVIEW

Gaining employment after graduation is a typical goal of many college students. Seeking opportunities in and out of class to develop abilities and skills can significantly increase your employment

Gaining experience in your field increases your marketability in the workplace as well as demonstrates your interest in and commitment to your field.

SELF-ASSESSMENT QUESTIONS

- What career-building activity most interests you?
- What steps do you need to take to begin your search for a career-building activity?

? CRITICAL THINKING QUESTION

▶ How can you determine the activities that are best suited to building your career?

opportunities. Having experience prior to beginning the job search can significantly increase your credibility and demonstrates commitment to your career choice. Career-building activities can include volunteer work, job shadowing, a part-time job, consulting work, or an internship. Through these activities, students can gain experience in utilizing both their technical, transferable, and soft skills.

CASE IN POINT: SKILLFUL SEARCH

Read the scenario below. Then, in groups or as a class, discuss the questions at the end.

In her last year of college, Alanna Phillips began to develop her resumé. During the process, Alanna analyzed her strengths and identified areas to develop. She discovered the following:

▶ Her college degree had given her a good start on developing the skills necessary for an entry-level job in her field.

▶ Development of some technical skills was still needed.

continued

continued

▶ Soft skills such as communication were effective but still could use some work.

▶ She had learned skills such as negotiating, delegating, and marketing but had no experience in utilizing these skills that could be documented on the resumé.

After reaching these conclusions, Alanna decided that gaining further experience using her skills was critical to obtaining the job she wanted after graduation. Alanna began to explore options for obtaining an internship.

▶ How can Alanna be sure that she has correctly identified her strengths and weaknesses?

▶ How can Alanna be sure that the skills learned in college are transferable to the workplace?

▶ What might Alanna do to identify more clearly what employers in her field are looking for when hiring entry-level employees?

▶ Would an internship help Alanna build on her skills? If so, how might she find out which internship would best benefit her needs and goals?

▶ What type of internship do you think would best serve Alanna's needs?

▶ How can an internship be helpful in promoting oneself to a prospective employer?

THE INTERNSHIP

In some professions, internships are commonly completed as part of the educational process as an option or, in some cases, as a requirement. Other names for internships include externship, onsite experience, or practicum. All refer to practical experience in the work setting. Loyola Marymount University Career Development Services (n.d., p. 1) defines an internship as "an experience whereby students learn to take on meaningful responsibilities within an organization and to adopt roles as contributing employees." Internships can take place at any time during the academic experience or as a capstone experience to classroom learning at the conclusion of academic preparation.

PURPOSE OF AN INTERNSHIP

According to McGill University Career and Placement Service (n.d., "Internships"), the purposes of an internship may include these:

▶ Learning more about a specific industry/field

▶ Gaining practical experience while applying theoretical knowledge

▶ Becoming more knowledgeable about specific work functions and learning career-related skills

▶ Gaining experience working with others and seeing how decisions are made

▶ Developing a relationship with a mentor and cultivating a network of contacts in your field

▶ Increasing your marketability

▶ Performing positive community service

▶ Gaining experience in job-seeking skills, interviewing, and resumé and cover letter preparation

▶ Getting to know yourself better

Making the most of an internship is the responsibility of the student. Maximizing learning from the internship experience requires involvement in the process of choosing the best internship possible for personal growth and development. Each student should be directly involved in the internship selection process, regardless of whether the internship is a requirement of the academic program. By being directly involved, the student can effectively meet individual goals. To determine individual internship goals, consider the following elements:

▶ **Your career interests.** Determine the areas of your field that are most interesting to you. Seek an internship that will provide you the opportunity to explore areas of interest. If you are unsure of your preference, an internship can help you define it by exposing you to various professional situations. Even if the internship is an academic requirement, do not consider it simply as another thing you have to do to graduate. Approach the experience with openness to learning as much as possible.

▶ **The internship environment.** Consider the environment in which you would like to complete your internship. Recall from Chapter 1 factors such as your goals, personality style, personal values, and the surroundings and atmosphere in which you like to work. Consider the size, philosophy, and other aspects of the potential internship site. Make sure the organization is a match with your internship goals and who you are as a person. Often success in an internship depends on the right fit.

▶ **Your current priorities.** Completing an internship requires the same level of commitment expected for a job. It is important to seek an internship experience that allows you to meet other life obligations. Consider the following aspects:

- **Location.** Whether you stay in your locale or travel across the country for an internship will depend largely on your other commitments. For example, an individual who has family responsibilities may choose not to accept an internship one thousand miles away, even though the internship site supports his interests and is a good fit. Conversely, another individual might make the opposite decision in the interest of gaining the experience. Making these types of decisions is frequently a part of selecting an internship site.

- **Finances.** Internships can be costly when they are full time (thus limiting available hours for paid employment) and when they have no stipend or other benefits. Benefits vary depending on the internship site. For example, a site might offer the intern a meal at the company cafeteria during her assigned shift. Other sites offer fully paid internships; still others offer a modest stipend. Be aware that paid internships of any kind are becoming less common. Some sites may be able to offer a part-time internship commitment to allow additional paid work hours. It is important to consider your financial priorities as part of internship selection.

- **Current employment.** If you intend to keep a paid job during your internship, it is important to negotiate a mutually acceptable plan with your employer. Taking a leave of

2

absence and modifying your hours are examples of solutions to balancing your paid work with an internship. Some employers may be able to consider you for a different position in your field upon completion of the internship.

LOCATING THE BEST INTERNSHIP

Once the goals of the internship have been established, the task of locating the best internship to meet those goals begins. If completion of an internship prior to graduation is a goal, then the search should begin as early in the academic process as possible, as an early search maximizes the chances that you will find the best internship to meet your needs. Some students may choose to do a different internship each year during their academic training, depending on the length of the academic program. The following are resources for locating an internship (R. S. Hansen, n.d.):

▶ **Career services office.** Nearly all career services offices have a list of their school's internship programs, important application dates, and other sources of internship information. The wide range of resources available in this office makes it an effective place to start your search. Some offices have an internship coordinator dedicated to locating internship sites.

▶ **Major/minor department.** Major-specific internship programs are frequently maintained by the department office. One or more faculty members may specifically handle internships.

▶ **Networking sources.** Tell everyone you know that you are looking for a specific type of internship. Just as with job hunting, face-to-face meetings and social networking are some of your best sources for internships, especially for competitive internships.

▶ **Internship and career fairs.** Most colleges offer at least one career fair during the academic year. Even if you are looking for an internship in a different geographic location, attend the fairs and network with the recruiters. Many organizations have multiple offices, and you may find an opportunity in your area of choice.

▶ **Alumni office.** Many colleges now ask alumni whether they would be willing to sponsor current college students as interns. These alums can be a source for internships as well as for networking opportunities.

◗ **Company web sites.** If you have already identified a specific set of companies where you would like to intern, consider researching them yourself by visiting the career section of each company's web site.

◗ **Internship web sites.** There are a few general internship web sites, as well as a number of industry-specific web sites. Conduct a search using the term "internships" or "internship AND (your field)" and explore your results.

◗ **Print resources.** Trade magazines, industry journals, and newspapers have advertisements from numerous organizations and companies. Reviewing journals can expose you to new organizations and aspects of your field.

◗ **Cold contact.** If other sources have not yielded results, then cold calling is an option. This process can involve calling contacts by phone or sending them an introduction letter to request further information.

apply it

Locating Internship Sites

GOAL: To demonstrate the ability to locate a variety of internship sites

STEP 1: Utilizing the resources suggested in this chapter, conduct research to locate at least three different possible internship sites. (Before doing this, check the protocol in your field. In some professions, internships are arranged strictly between academic staff and site supervisors. If you are in this category, involve your internship coordinator in this activity.)

STEP 2: After locating an internship, call or write to the company to inquire whether an internship is available and what the company's requirements are. Ask for guidance during this process as needed.

STEP 3: Put together a brief report of findings to present to the instructor.

STEP 4: Consider placing the information from locating internship sites in your Learning Portfolio.

2

SELF-ASSESSMENT QUESTIONS

• What resources do you think you would find the most useful in locating an internship?
• What resource do you not feel comfortable using but believe could be worthwhile? How can you become more comfortable using this resource?
• How do you think you can document your search efforts for an internship? How might this documentation be helpful to you now and in your future job search activities?

CRITICAL THINKING QUESTION

◗ How would you adjust your research tactics if you were trying to locate part-time work, consulting work, or a shadowing experience?

2

Once a number of possible internship sites have been identified, it is important to remain diligent in following through with the necessary calls and letters. Being persistent is important and can make a difference in whether you obtain the desired internship. Be sensitive to the employer's time, and contact employers only when absolutely necessary during this process. Preparing well-written resumés, cover letters, and thank-you letters for the internship search is also important.

INTERNSHIP SUCCESS

Success of an internship is up to the employer *and* the student. If academic credit is to be received for the internship, then the college can also be instrumental in helping to ensure that the internship experience is a success. School personnel can facilitate communication between the site supervisor and the student by initiating requests for necessary documents such as internship time sheets and site supervisor evaluation reports. Ultimately, it is the student's responsibility to follow up and ensure that required tasks and forms are completed and to make his or her internship a beneficial experience.

Certain actions and attitudes on your part will contribute to your learning and success. Maximize the benefits you gain from your internship experience by implementing the following recommendations:

It is the student's responsibility to communicate effectively with the internship supervisor and to demonstrate the same professional skills that will be expected on the job.

▶ **Be informed.** Knowing what is expected of you by both the school and the internship site is critical to your success. Prior to arriving at the internship site, learn as much as you can about dress codes, schedules, policies, and other relevant aspects of the job. An introductory meeting or telephone call to the internship supervisor or coordinator offers an opportunity for you to introduce yourself as well as ask questions and get relevant information. You are also likely to have an orientation session upon your arrival at the site.

If your internship is part of your academic requirements, there will be standards set by your school or program that you will have to meet. Examples are deadlines for submitting paperwork (which can have a direct influence on your grade or ability to graduate on time) and performance requirements for grades. The internship coordinator on your campus will be able to provide you with relevant information. Be sure to ask questions if anything is unclear.

Stockbyte/Getty Images

▶ **Prepare.** Learning as much as possible about the site prior to your arrival will facilitate your transition to the site. For example, learn about the expectations of your role and the types of clients with whom you will work. Learn about the organization and its history. Being prepared will increase your comfort level as you begin your internship, as well as demonstrate your initiative and interest.

▶ **Treat the internship as you would a new job.** The internship is where you make your debut into the professional world. Demonstrate the same commitment and investment that you would if you were starting a new job. The internship is similar to a first job and is the ideal place to develop positive professional habits. In addition, internships are frequently listed on the resumé as work experience, and you may be using your internship supervisor as a professional reference. Many interns are hired by the internship site either at the conclusion of the internship or later in their careers.

▶ **Be inquisitive and open to learning.** Demonstrate an interest in your work, the organization's activities, and other events related to the internship site. Be open to learning about new ideas and trying new things. Ask questions. Your interest demonstrates dedication to your work and the organization and a willingness to grow professionally.

▶ **Take responsibility.** The step beyond being inquisitive is to actively seek opportunities for learning. Find organizational and professional activities of interest and become involved rather than waiting to be asked. Be accountable for your actions.

▶ **Use supervision to your benefit.** You will probably have regular meetings with your supervisor to discuss your progress and to discuss any issues that might arise. Use supervision to ask questions, clarify information, and explore areas of interest. Pressing issues should be addressed immediately, but supervision is the appropriate venue for discussion and fostering professional development. Use positive feedback to develop your strengths; accept constructive criticism to set goals for growth and improvement.

▶ **Use your critical thinking skills.** Think through problems and issues objectively and thoroughly. Avoid personal bias and emotional responses that cloud professional judgment. Analyze data and base decisions on rational and verifiable

2

information. Act on ethical principles and in the best interest of clients and the organization.

▶ **Respect professional boundaries and limits in a positive way.** All professionals—including seasoned ones—have limits to their knowledge and expertise. All professionals have room for growth and development. Recognizing what you *don't* know is as important as recognizing your strengths. If there is something you don't know or understand, ask for clarification or assistance, and in doing so, be sure that your attitude reflects your desire to learn. Do not use not knowing or not understanding as an excuse for not doing a task. Likewise, professional roles have boundaries. For example, a health aide cannot administer medications, even though she might know how. Medication is administered by a nurse, for regulatory and safety reasons. These types of professional boundaries are in place for liability and management reasons. Understand your professional boundaries, recognize why they exist, and respect them.

▶ **Pay attention to professional behaviors and standards.** Chapter 1 emphasized the importance of professional ethics and standards. It is your responsibility to know and apply these guidelines to your internship responsibilities. Maintain your awareness of these standards and consciously apply them to your decisions and actions. For example, if you are unsure about the "right" way to approach a problem that arises in your work, consider your professional code of ethics in addition to technical solutions. Consider whether your technical solution is acceptable from an ethical perspective.

▶ **Respect and fit into the organization's culture. Be a team player.** Participate in activities that contribute to a positive environment and work relationships. You might choose one or two activities that are suited to your interests and comfort level. It is important to be visible in your organization in a positive way.

▶ **Create tangible results.** Strive to create materials or processes of substance that can be listed as accomplishments on a resumé or professional portfolio. This may be anything from creating marketing materials, to conducting industry research, to organizing a client meeting, and so on. Prospective employers will note your specific contributions to the organization. This helps you to stand out among the other applicants.

SELF-ASSESSMENT QUESTIONS

- What is your response to positive feedback? How can you use it to develop your professional strengths and skills?
- What is your typical response to constructive criticism? How can you use it to set goals and improve areas needing development?

❓ CRITICAL THINKING QUESTION

▶ How would you respond if you were asked to do something that was clearly outside of your professional boundaries?

SELF-ASSESSMENT QUESTION

- What will you do to ensure success in your internship experience?

success steps for internship success

- Be informed.
- Prepare.
- Treat the internship as you would a new job.
- Be inquisitive and open to learning.
- Take responsibility.
- Use supervision to your benefit.
- Use your critical thinking skills.
- Respect professional boundaries and limits in a positive way.
- Pay attention to professional behaviors and standards.
- Respect and fit into the organization's culture.
- Create tangible results.

apply it

Internship Site Visit Report

GOAL: To gain a better understanding of the requirements of an internship site

STEP 1: Groups of four or five students are each given information for a prearranged internship site visit. The site should be different for each group.

STEP 2: When visiting the site, students document what is learned about the site, how interns function at that site, and the site's requirements for interns. Students also inquire into what makes a good intern versus a poor intern.

STEP 3: After the visit, group members compile their information and prepare a brief report to present to the class.

STEP 4: Consider putting this report in your Learning Portfolio.

LEVERAGING YOUR INTERNSHIP WITH PROSPECTIVE EMPLOYERS

In this difficult job market and lackluster economy, it is important to leverage your internship experience with any prospective employer. By doing so, you stand a better chance of landing another internship

2

or perhaps even a job. Hughes (2010) offers the following tips on how to use your internship to its greatest advantage:

▶ **When finished with a project, ask for more.** Show your worth. Going beyond what is asked of you shows initiative and demonstrates your skill set. It will also likely lead to a strong recommendation once the internship is completed. In some instances, an internship may turn into a full-time position postgraduation.

▶ **Keep in touch with past internship employers.** If you had a positive work experience at an internship, make the effort to stay in touch with past internship supervisors. They and former coworkers may be able to help you network for future job opportunities.

▶ **Conduct informational interviews.** This is one of the most important networking tools available today. Informational interviews are covered in detail in Chapter 3.

CHAPTER SUMMARY

This chapter emphasized the importance of recognizing both your strengths and areas needing development and then setting goals for professional development in preparation for the job search. You were encouraged to begin this process as early as possible by assuming leadership roles on and off campus, researching and becoming involved in your profession, and networking with individuals in your field. Completing an internship was discussed as a significant means to enter your field and gain experience in the workplace. You reviewed important phases of the internship, including selecting, preparing for, and completing the internship, and you were provided with guidelines for the successful completion of each of the three phases. Finally, you were given some tips on how to leverage your internship with prospective employers.

POINTS TO KEEP IN MIND

In this chapter, several main points were discussed in detail:

▶ To be successful and competitive within your profession requires having well-defined goals.

▶ Technical skills are those that are necessary to perform specific job tasks.

▶ Transferable skills are the type of skills that can be easily transferred to another job or work setting.

▶ Self-assessment inventories can provide individuals with insight into their interests, skills, and personality type.

▶ Self-assessment tools include the Strong Interest Inventory, MBTI, TypeFocus, and the SAI.

▶ Gaining experience can provide more credibility and demonstrates commitment to one's career choice. This experience can come through obtaining a part-time job, performing volunteer work, engaging in job shadowing, doing consulting work, or completing an internship.

▶ Being directly involved in the internship selection process can help to ensure your goals are met.

▶ There are a variety of resources available to obtain an internship. These sources include web sites, books, periodicals, and school officials.

▶ It is up to you, the student, to make the internship experience benefit your future professional success.

CHECK YOUR UNDERSTANDING

Visit www.cengagebrain.com to see how well you have mastered the material in Chapter 2.

SUGGESTED ITEMS FOR LEARNING PORTFOLIO

▶ Self-Assessment Questions: Include your written responses to these questions. Use them to review your development over time.

▶ Self-Assessment Test: Keep a record of what you discovered about yourself.

2

▶ Locating Internship Sites: Find and research potential internship sites.

▶ Internship Site Visit Report: Prepare a report on internship requirements at a particular site.

REFERENCES

Bruce, C. (n.d.). Career advice for engineering & other technical majors. The Black Collegian Online. Retrieved February 22, 2013, from http://www.blackcollegian.com/career-advice-for-engineering-other -technical-majors/

Dikel, M. R. (2002). A guide to choosing tests that are right for you [Electronic version]. Retrieved February 25, 2013, from the Dow Jones Career Journal web site: http://www.career-intelligence.com/pdf_files /Career_Journal_2.pdf

Hansen, K. (n.d.). Strategic portrayal of transferable job skills is a vital job search technique. Retrieved February 22, 2013, from http://www .quintcareers.com/transferable_skills_technique.html

Hansen, R. S. (n.d.). How to find your ideal internship: A Three-Step Process for Gaining Key Work Experience While in College. Retrieved February 25, 2013, from http://www.quintcareers.com/finding_ideal _internship.html

Hughes, C. (2010). Leveraging internships. American University Career Center. Retrieved February 25, 2013, from http://aucareercenter .wordpress.com/2010/07/20/leveraging-internships/

Klaus, P. (n.d.). Are you up to snuff when it comes to soft skills? Retrieved February 22, 2013, from http://www.quintcareers.com/job-seeker _soft_skills.html

Loyola Marymount University, Career Development Services. (n.d.). What is an LMU internship? Retrieved February 25, 2013, from http://www .lmu.edu/AssetFactory.aspx?vid=30395

McGill University, Career and Placement Service. (n.d.). Internships Retrieved February 25, 2013, from http://www.mcgill.ca/caps /students/job/internship

University of California, Berkeley—Career Center. (n.d.). Evaluate yourself. Retrieved February 25, 2013, from https://career.berkeley.edu/Plan /FOCUS-2.stm

part 2

Tools for the Job Search

Part II of *100% Job Search Success* identifies the tools needed to aid in a successful job search.

Chapter 3: Networking and Self-Promotion describes how the use of traditional and social networking and personal branding are means to develop professional contacts within your field.

Chapter 4: Resumé and Cover Letter Development provides the foundations for preparing a resumé, cover letter, and other types of professional correspondence used during the job search process.

Chapter 5: Developing a Professional Portfolio introduces you to professional portfolios as a tool for showcasing your professional skills and achievements.

Chapter 6: Professionalism in the Job Search focuses on professionalism and acceptable etiquette in the job search process.

3

Networking and Self-Promotion

LEARNING OBJECTIVES

By the end of this chapter, you will achieve the following objectives:

- ▶ Define *traditional networking* and describe what it is not.
- ▶ Describe the purposes of traditional networking.
- ▶ Describe various traditional networking venues and how each is best utilized.
- ▶ Practice steps of effective traditional networking in various settings.
- ▶ Implement strategies to increase the effectiveness of traditional networking.
- ▶ Define social networking.
- ▶ Describe the purposes of social networking.
- ▶ Describe various social networking opportunities.
- ▶ Define personal branding and identify strategies for its use.
- ▶ Implement additional networking techniques.

BE IN THE KNOW

Card Shark

As you will learn, networking business cards are a great way to advertise yourself if you are just graduating or looking to change careers. Use these templates below to get you started on designing your own cards. Examples of networking business cards can be found by doing an Internet search. Printing shops will also have examples for you to review.

The investment is minimal to produce these cards—often just $10 for 250 cards.

Front of Card

| NAME |
| Positioning Statement (4–6 words) |
| • Key Strength 1   • Key Strength 4 |
| • Key Strength 2   • Key Strength 5 |
| • Key Strength 3   • Key Strength 6 |
| |
| E-MAIL   PHONE |
| LinkedIn Profile |

Back of Card

| CAREER OBJECTIVES |
| Title: |
| Function: |
| Industry: |
| Geography: |
| Target Companies: |

TRADITIONAL NETWORKING

There are many definitions and descriptions of traditional networking. "Networking is about meeting people...and finding that person or persons who has an interest in your skills, background, and what you can bring to a company" (Kovar, n.d.[a]). Essentially, networking is establishing relationships and contacts, sustained over time, that benefit both parties in the professional world. In the case of seeking job referrals and a niche in the professional workplace, networking is typically directed at establishing relationships that can lead to employment opportunities and professional growth.

Briefly, networking involves meeting people who can provide you with pertinent information and referrals and to whom you can provide the same or something comparable. Obtaining information and getting referrals may involve face-to-face meetings, telephone conversations, or e-mail correspondence (Kovar, n.d.[b]). The remainder of this chapter will focus on how to engage in successful traditional and social networking and personal branding techniques to enhance your job search efforts and professional contacts.

WHAT TRADITIONAL NETWORKING IS *NOT*

Effectively describing traditional networking may begin with an explanation of what it is not. Several sources describe common misconceptions of networking. Networking is not any of the following:

- Calling the people you know when you need a job (Flantzer, n.d.). You may get lucky using this approach, but results are not likely to be as effective or long term as they can be with true networking.

- Telling people how wonderful you are (Bjorseth, as cited in Kovar, n.d.[b]). Although a part of networking does involve promoting yourself and your skills, self-promotion is directed at demonstrating how your skills can meet the needs and support goal achievement of others.

- Getting a referral from everyone you talk to (Kovar, n.d.[b]). You can expect a certain number of rejections and/or individuals who are unable or unwilling to assist you in your networking efforts. Effective networking takes time, patience, and persistence.

- All about you (Kovar, n.d.[a]; Flantzer, n.d.; Kurow, 2010). Although you are likely to benefit from networking, it also involves giving support to others. Networking relationships are mutually beneficial. You must add value to your networking relationships by giving in return to people you meet during the networking process.

Professional networking results in mutually beneficial relationships in which you give and receive information that supports professional development.

WHAT TRADITIONAL NETWORKING IS

Networking is the establishment and maintenance of mutually supportive professional relationships over time. Establishing a network to belong to that provides mutually beneficial results takes time, commitment, and attention. Networking means having relationships with a variety of people who can provide information and resources to each other. Consider the following aspects of successful networking, recommended by Kovar (n.d.[b]):

- **Networking occurs over a sustained time period.** It is unlikely that you will achieve a lead for employment (or other information) during a single contact or at one particular

3

time. Patience and persistence are necessary for successful networking. Establishing the effective relationships upon which successful networking is built requires time as well as maintaining contact with the individual.

▶ **Successful networking requires courtesy and respect.**
Courtesy and consideration are of paramount importance in professional networking. You demonstrate consideration in part by being respectful of busy schedules, offering something of value in return, demonstrating effective listening skills, and expressing appreciation.

▶ **Research and knowledge are critical elements of networking.**
It is important to research the industry or organization in which you have interest or with which your contact is involved. Kovar (n.d.[b]) suggests the Internet as a tool for conducting effective research. Refer to Chapter 1 for an in-depth discussion on conducting company- and field-specific research.

THE PURPOSE OF TRADITIONAL NETWORKING

Networking can serve a variety of purposes. Although as a college student your main focus for networking is likely to be finding employment, keep in mind that the concepts of networking can be applied to a variety of situations and may serve you well at various times throughout your career. The following purposes of networking are adapted from Flantzer (n.d.):

▶ **Networking provides knowledge.** If you have a working knowledge of your field and its trends, you are more likely to be prepared to present yourself effectively to potential employers. Also, if corporate downsizing affects you at some time in your career, current knowledge of trends in your field will prepare you to be more aware of your options.

▶ **Networking provides contacts for employment.**
Networking puts you in contact with individuals who may be able to hire you or refer you to a potential employer. Use your knowledge of your field to present yourself as informed and skilled. Networking provides the opportunity for you to communicate how your skills can benefit a potential employer's organization.

◗ **Networking establishes mutually beneficial relationships.**
The networking process also introduces you to individuals who might benefit from your connections and knowledge and with whom you can establish mutually beneficial relationships. By positioning yourself in a way that allows you to help others, you set the stage for exchanging information that can benefit you and your contacts. Professional organizations are excellent resources for obtaining current industry knowledge, as well as for making professional contacts.

TRADITIONAL NETWORKING OPPORTUNITIES

In general terms, traditional networking opportunities manifest themselves through activities that exist, or activities that you (and perhaps others) create. Existing opportunities include contacting established businesses and organizations where your skills might be needed. Networks that you create might include contacts that you make at networking or social events and that represent a wide variety of organizations.

EXISTING NETWORKS

Using an existing network means going to an event sponsored by a specific organization or conducting an informational interview with an individual at the organization (informational interviews are discussed later in this chapter). Utilizing an existing network offers a more focused approach to networking but may not present the diversity that created networks can provide. Existing networks are most useful when you are pursuing a position in a specific organization or seeking a niche in a particular field. The following are examples of existing networks:

◗ An existing business or organization
◗ An industry-specific career fair
◗ Your field's professional organization(s)

CREATED NETWORKS

Created networks are those that you develop from a wide variety of sources. For example, you may attend a social event and a conference and go to dinner with friends in another industry. You establish a relationship with an individual from each of these venues. You follow up appropriately and take the steps to maintain effective networking

3

©Istockphoto.com/Mediaphotos

Networks can be created and developed from a variety of social and business settings.

relationships (these steps will be discussed later in this chapter). By taking these steps, you have created a network. Created networks may take longer and more energy to establish than existing networks but can be richer in what they can offer because of their diversity. They are most useful for someone who wishes to explore different fields, is looking for a change, or would like to apply his or her skills in a new area. Created networks can be formed from any activity or venue where you are interacting with other people. Some of the more formal venues include these:

▶ Non-industry-specific career fairs

▶ Professional organizations outside of your field

▶ Networking groups and mixers

▶ Chamber of Commerce events

STEPS IN THE TRADITIONAL NETWORKING PROCESS

Incorporating the elements of successful networking can be accomplished by following basic steps and organizing your endeavors around those steps. The following are steps of the traditional networking process as it relates specifically to the job search process from Bguides .com (2005).

▌ **Have a networking plan.** Know what you are seeking and have a goal in mind. Clarify the information you need and steps you need to take to achieve your objective. Know the types of people who can provide you with valuable information, and seek to meet those individuals. Determine the types of settings and events where you can best achieve this. From this information, devise a plan for your networking.

▌ **Be aware of and prepared for networking opportunities as they present themselves (often in unexpected places).** It is important to be prepared for networking opportunities as they present themselves. You are more likely to recognize opportunities when you have prepared an effective networking plan. Based on your plan, be prepared with a personal introduction, questions that will engage the individual and encourage conversation, open-ended questions that will lead to the information you are seeking, and a closing statement that expresses appreciation for the person's time and information. You may or may not request an opportunity for follow-up.

▌ **Put yourself in situations where you will meet people.** Effective networking requires interaction with others. Involve yourself in activities where you are likely to meet new people. Activities can be professional or social.

▌ **Communicate effectively.** Effective communication requires skillful nonverbal and verbal messages. Be aware of how others perceive your facial expressions, eye contact, general energy level (which should not be too low and yet not overwhelming), and gestures. Rely on your plan and the questions you have prepared to sound polished and professional. (Avoid sounding like a recording.) Use effective listening skills and ask pertinent, open-ended questions. Remember that both nonverbal and verbal communication can have different meanings to individuals from diverse cultures. Be sensitive to cultural preferences and perceptions.

▌ **Develop quality relationships.** The key to effective networking is the quality of relationships rather than the quantity of

Networking can occur in any situation, including those where you might not expect it. For example, social events and informal gatherings can present excellent networking opportunities.

Photodisc/Getty Images

relationships. Keep your goals in mind so that you can foster relationships that support them. Quality relationships are based on developing a mutual understanding of individual needs and goals and providing information that supports them. Remember to add value to your relationships by giving back.

▶ **Stay organized and support individuals who assist you.** Be organized. After you meet someone, make notes regarding his or her affiliation, expertise, and interests, along with other pertinent information about your meeting. In addition to supporting your goals, you will have information about the person and may be able to offer something related to his or her interests and goals.

▶ **Follow up appropriately.** It is essential to follow up any networking activity with a handwritten thank-you note. Thank your contacts for referrals, information, and other assistance that they provide. It is also courteous to express appreciation for someone's time and effort, even if no specific referrals or leads came from the information. If you are in doubt regarding whether to send a thank-you note, it is best to err on the side of sending one. Expressing appreciation is always acceptable.

▶ **Enjoy yourself and have fun with the networking process.** Meeting people is fun and can support your current interests as well as spark new ones. You may discover new aspects of yourself or your profession. Approach networking with an open mind and a spirit of adventure.

success steps for traditional networking

- Have a networking plan.
- Be aware of and prepared for networking opportunities as they present themselves (often in unexpected places).
- Put yourself in situations where you will meet people.
- Communicate effectively.
- Develop quality relationships.
- Stay organized and support individuals who assist you.
- Follow up appropriately.

apply it

A Networking Plan

GOAL: To establish a plan for successful networking

STEP 1: On a sheet of paper or in an electronic document, list the elements of preparing to network. These steps, adapted from Bguides.com (2005), include the following:

a. your goal

b. steps you need to take to achieve your objective

c. information you need

d. types of people you need to meet

e. types of settings and events where you might meet these people

STEP 2: From your list, and based on the resources available in your locale, determine specific networking venues, identify people who fit the types you have defined, and research information that you will need to be well prepared.

STEP 3: In preparation for actually networking, record contact information for individuals and registration information for events.

MAXIMIZING YOUR TRADITIONAL NETWORKING SUCCESS

Sustaining relationships over time requires investment of time and energy. In today's busy world, it is unreasonable to expect that someone you have met briefly will remember you. However, if you have stayed in touch and given back it may be more likely that people will think of you when they encounter someone who might be helpful to you. Consider the following suggestions for maintaining your visibility with the contacts that you make:

▶ **Make others feel valued.** Pay attention to contacts' accomplishments and attributes that merit recognition. Give sincere compliments and respect for achievement and successes.

▶ **Demonstrate thoughtfulness.** Considerate actions can make an impression. Gestures that are done in another's best interest and without expectation for reward are typically appreciated and remembered. If you have done and organized your networking notes on the contacts you have made, this should be a fairly easy task.

▸ **Stay connected.** Schulzke (2010) emphasizes the importance of staying in touch with people to keep the relationship going. For example, you can pass along anything of interest to your contacts, but make sure it is professional in meaning and something that they would feel is value-added. You can also remember special occasions such as birthdays or business events. To get the most out of the relationship, the author suggests that you touch base with your contacts at least twice a year. People are flattered that you included them in your correspondence, and doing so keeps your name in front of them.

▸ **Focus on what you can offer others.** Let your contacts know what you can bring to their organization. Kurow (2010) reminds us that people are typically most interested in how you can help them. Maintain a clear picture of the contributions you can make based on your skills and talents and be able to express how these meet your contacts' needs. Use what you have learned in your research to understand your contacts' needs and be prepared to demonstrate how you can help them.

▸ **Get involved.** Volunteering is an excellent way to expand your contacts in a field (Rangwala, n.d.). Join a club or committee that interests you and that gives you the opportunity to meet new contacts.

? **CRITICAL THINKING QUESTION**

▸ How can you begin to implement networking steps and activities to create a strong network for your job search?

success steps for maximizing your networking success

- Make others feel valued.
- Demonstrate thoughtfulness.
- Stay connected.
- Focus on what you can offer others.
- Get involved.

apply it

Networking Preparation

GOAL: To prepare for effective networking

STEP 1: Prepare a list of topics related to your field on which you would like information. Also, prepare a brief introduction of yourself and your goals.

STEP 2: Prepare a list of open-ended questions related to your topics that would be appropriately asked of a networking contact. If you need help with questions, conduct an Internet search using "professional networking" as your search term and look for articles that suggest effective open-ended questions.

STEP 3: Familiarize yourself with the questions you decide on so that you are comfortable and effective using them when the appropriate situation arises.

STEP 4: Practice with classmates, friends, or other individuals who will give you honest and constructive feedback.

apply it

Simulated Networking

GOAL: To practice presenting yourself effectively during a networking opportunity

STEP 1: Set aside a time with classmates to hold a "networking event." You may set this up as part of a class activity or as an event held after school hours either on or off campus. You may find it effective to involve other students by requesting the assistance of your career services department.

STEP 2: Make appropriate arrangements according to the plans you have made.

STEP 3: Attend the event as you would any other networking event. Practice the steps outlined in this chapter and use them during the event.

STEP 4: Although this is a *simulated* activity, be aware of opportunities that can present themselves. Remember that opportunities can be found anywhere.

CASE IN POINT: IT'S NOT WHAT YOU KNOW BUT WHO YOU KNOW

Read the scenario below. Then, in groups or as a class, discuss the questions at the end.

Roger McPherson is a recent graduate about ready to enter the professional job ranks for the first time. As he was beginning his search, a career counselor

continued

continued

told him that many advertised jobs are filled long before they are posted in print or on the Internet. The career counselor told him that the best way to jump-start his career was to use traditional and social networking techniques to make connections in the field as a way to promote himself effectively.

▶ What did the career counselor mean by "traditional networking" and "social networking"?

▶ What did the career counselor mean when he told Roger to "promote himself effectively"?

▶ Where are some places that Roger might begin his networking?

▶ What are some important points for Roger to remember as he begins networking?

▶ How should Roger organize his networking efforts?

SOCIAL NETWORKING

Webopedia (2010a) defines a social network as a "social structure made of nodes that are generally individuals or organizations. A social network represents relationships and flows between people, groups, organizations, animals, computers or other information/knowledge processing entities." Webopedia (2010b) further defines a social networking site (SNS) as "any Web site that enables users to create public profiles within that Web site and form relationships with other users of the same Web site who access their profile. Social networking sites can be used to describe community-based Web sites, online discussions, forums, chatrooms, and other social spaces online."

PURPOSE OF SOCIAL NETWORKING

Social networking has many purposes. Many social networking sites link individuals with common interests, such as politics, religion, or hobbies. Other sites, such as Facebook, give people the opportunity to share information with their friends. In recent years, the whole concept of social networking has been embraced by the business and professional worlds as a means to conduct business, seek employment, and build professional associations among individuals.

As you have seen, starting a job search is not an easy task. Job search expert Kevin Donlin (n.d.) says that most jobs are in the "hidden job market"—those jobs that are found through networking and internal recommendations. He recommends social networking as a great tool to use when conducting a job search.

USING SOCIAL NETWORKING IN THE JOB SEARCH

These days, successful job searching is becoming as sophisticated as the technology that drives the process. Not only is this true for the job seeker, but it is true for the job recruiter as well. Consider these statistics provided by Jobvite, a software applications company that manages all aspects of the hiring process, including recruiting practices. In its Social Recruiting Survey 2012, hiring firms report that:

- 92% use or plan to use social recruiting
- 43% of recruiters who use social recruiting saw an increase in candidate quality
- 73% have successfully hired a candidate through social media
- 31% of recruiters using social media have seen a sustained increase in employee referrals (Jobvite 2012[b]).

So, as a soon-to-be or recent college graduate, what strategies can you employ in your job search that leverages social networking as a viable (and increasingly critical) job searching tool?

BUILD YOUR PROFESSIONAL ONLINE REPUTATION

One of the most important strategies you can employ when embarking on a social networking path is that of building a professional online reputation. A professional online reputation is your "public business persona," as seen by those who share in your social networking activities on sites such as Facebook, LinkedIn, and Twitter.

With upwards of 86% of recruiters accessing candidate social profiles during the job search, it is imperative that the information you post on all social networking sites presents you in the best possible business light (Jobvite 2012[b]). A positive social networking profile also aids in making and keeping business connections and helps to formulate your personal "brand" that distinguishes you from the crowd (read more about personal branding later in this chapter).

The following are strategies for building a professional online reputation:

▶ **Choose your colleagues wisely.** Affiliate yourself with people who you hope will recommend you and that you will recommend to others.

▶ **Share and share alike.** What you know can not only help your cause, but the cause of others. If you have nonproprietary information that might be of value to your contacts, share it. This creates value in your network and helps further identify your personal brand.

▶ **One picture is worth…trouble?** Commenting on blogs and uploading pictures leaves a permanent trail of you, good or bad. Don't leave yourself open to public viewing—and scrutiny—by posting *anything* of a questionable nature.

▶ **Think before you tweet.** Don't let your personal comments cross your professional boundaries. Remember, most employers check social profiles during the job search process.

▶ **Don't let your (online) reputation precede you.** Keep your personal and professional information current, accurate, and interesting. A negative perception of you, whether warranted or not, will follow you indefinitely (Bryan, E. C. n.d.).

SOCIAL NETWORKING PROFILES

As a young adult, the chances are very high that you are already an active participant in social networking in some capacity. You may "tweet" with friends and strangers on Twitter, ask friends and family to "like" you on Facebook, or "pin" images, videos, and other objects of interest on Pinterest.

As a young adult who is also a job seeker, the use of social networking takes on additional meaning and personal responsibility. According to the Jobvite 2012 Social Job Seeker Survey, 88% of all job seekers have at least one social networking profile, 64% have two, and 44% have three profiles (Jobvite 2012[a]).

Social networking and social networking profiles continue to gain ground and credibility in the entire job search process for both seekers and employers. Note the following statistics from the Jobvite 2012 Social Job Seeker Survey:

▶ **Facebook.** 52% of job seekers use Facebook to help find work, and 49% use Facebook contacts for career gain.

▶ **LinkedIn.** 38% of job seekers use LinkedIn to help find work and use those contacts for career gain.

▶ **Twitter.** 34% of job seekers use Twitter to help find work, and 35% use Twitter contacts for career gain (Jobvite 2012[a]).

Regardless of which social networking site(s) you use, choose your postings wisely. Let social media help you in your job search, not hurt you.

PERSONAL BRANDING

Most of us probably only think of the term *brand* when it comes to a product or service. You may also associate it with "brand name," as in Kleenex instead of tissue, Band-Aid instead of bandage, or Pepsi instead of cola. A brand, if well promoted, is instantly recognizable in both its designation and its reputation. That reputation may include such criteria as consistency, reliability, availability, price, trustworthiness, and identity, to name a few.

The concept of branding goes beyond products and services that we purchase, however. Branding also encompasses the job search process. In effect, *personal branding* is your reputation as a job candidate and employee.

PERSONAL BRANDING DEFINED

Meg Guiseppi, a certified Personal Branding, Resume, and Job Search Strategist, says "personal branding is about defining and knowing what makes you unique and valuable to the employers you're targeting, and clearly communicating your value proposition and good-fit qualities for your target employers when you network and interview for jobs" (Guiseppi, 2012).

Guiseppi adds that personal branding can highlight your "softer" skills that might mesh well with an organization. Today's employers

❓ CRITICAL THINKING QUESTION

▶ How many social networking profiles do you have? Do you think you use them wisely when it comes to your job search?

3

3

seek candidates who not only bring technical skills and knowledge to the position, but those who also fit within the corporate culture. Personal branding can serve as a differentiator that works in your favor (Guiseppi 2010).

STRATEGIES FOR BUILDING A PERSONAL BRAND

Most job seekers do not take the time to assess, or are unaware of, the importance of creating a personal brand. They are hopeful that their words and actions alone will help them "stand out in a crowd" and that they will be rewarded with a job or promotion simply based on those criteria.

Savvy job seekers, on the other hand, do recognize the value that a personal brand can bring to the job search process. The following are some strategies for building and strengthening your personal brand.

▶ **Your brand starts with your accomplishments.** Take stock of your successes to date, including both personal and professional. As you move forward, think about what you want your brand to stand for and then seek out new experiences that support that image. For example, if you are still in school, search for one or more internships that tie into your career path. If you are already working, think about volunteering, outside consulting, or freelancing in addition to your current position.

▶ **Assess your level of education and training.** Depending upon your field, you may be required to have a certain level of education, training, or certifications in order to be employed. To further identify your personal brand, try to broaden your education, whether formally or informally. Consider attending seminars and conferences or writing scholarly papers that address issues related to your field. Some employers offer tuition reimbursement that can lead to an advanced degree.

▶ **Market yourself.** No one knows your brand any better than you do. Take the time to strategically advertise your selling points to others by creating your own web site, professional portfolio, or other online presence. Be sure that your information is current and relatable to your field. Creativity counts, but not as much as maintaining a professional stance.

Constant contact. Do not let your personal brand become stagnant. Continue to grow your relationships and build your network beyond what it is today. Your skills continue to strengthen and evolve—make sure that your personal brand does as well (Hansen, n.d.[a]).

OTHER NETWORKING TECHNIQUES

There are other techniques that can add to your networking skills. Networking opportunities can present themselves at any time, and you will have to be prepared. Other situations may require a more formal approach. Methods that you can use in both of these circumstances are presented here.

THE ELEVATOR SPEECH

An elevator speech is a "short (15–30 second, 150-word) sound bite that succinctly and memorably introduces you" (Kurow, 2010). The term *elevator speech* is derived from the idea that you should be able to deliver your introduction and make a lasting impression in the time it takes to ride an elevator. Elevator speeches are also sometimes called "30-second commercials." You should highlight your unique qualities and their benefits in your elevator speech, and do so in an assured and conversational manner.

You can use your elevator speech anytime and anywhere you wish to introduce yourself to a potential contact and spark his or her interest. Typically, you can use your elevator speech when anyone asks you the question, "What do you do?" Elevator speeches can be used in a variety of settings from formal networking events to standing in line at the grocery store. Kurow (2010) makes the following suggestions for devising an elevator speech:

▶ **Consider the benefits that you can deliver.** You are more likely to evoke interest if your elevator speech clearly identifies the benefits of what you do. The advantages you can deliver are likely to capture the attention of your contact and lead to further conversation. List all your services and their benefits.

3

> ## success steps for creating an elevator speech
>
> - Consider the benefits that you can deliver.
> - Create a captivating opening line based on benefits.
> - Practice!

▶ **Create a captivating opening line based on benefits.** Your opening line should capture attention as well as raise the listener's curiosity. The listener should want to hear more. For example, a woman who sells jewelry might say, "I'm Suzanne Smith, and I help women to shine and sparkle." It is not necessary to include your title in your opening line.

▶ **Practice!** Your elevator speech should flow easily. Practice your speech until you come across as confident, sincere, and engaging.

THE INFORMATIONAL INTERVIEW

The informational interview is conducted to obtain information about a field or specific company. It is more formal than networking and chance encounters in that it is a scheduled appointment for which you must thoughtfully prepare. The Career Center at Florida

apply it

Elevator Speech Preparation

GOAL: To prepare an effective elevator speech

STEP 1: Individually, follow the steps for preparing an elevator speech listed in this chapter. Prepare several introductory statements that are engaging, summarize the benefits of your skills, and stimulate further interest.

STEP 2: After individuals have prepared their elevator speeches, gather in small groups and share your speeches. Share feedback and suggestions for improvement. You may find ways to combine the statements that you have prepared to make an even greater impact.

STEP 3: Practice your elevator speech with a classmate until you can deliver it smoothly and effectively.

State University (2007) and Crosby (2002) list the following purposes of the informational interview:

▶ Gaining information about a career or profession

▶ Gaining information about a specific organization

▶ Improving your general interviewing skills and ability to communicate with a variety of professionals

▶ Using the interview as a networking tool to broaden your base of professional contacts

▶ Gaining insight into the realities of the workplace

▶ Learning effective methods of preparing for a specific career

▶ Discovering new careers and fields that may be of interest

Steps in Informational Interviewing

The steps of an informational interview are similar to preparing for networking opportunities. Research, question preparation, and courteous professional skills are all of paramount importance. Consider the following steps for preparing a productive informational interview, adapted from Crosby (2002):

▶ **Do your research.** As was the case with networking, effective research will provide you with a strong basis for your interviewing and will allow you to ask more effective questions and acquire more in-depth information. Consider professional organizations, instructors, and the career placement department at your school as sources for your research.

▶ **Select a person to interview.** Your research sources may also be able to suggest individuals to interview. Consider the following considerations when selecting a person to interview:

• Select individuals in the field in which you are interested. Crosby points out that these individuals will know more about your field than human resource personnel do.

• Select individuals who have approximately the same level of responsibility that you would have upon entry into the field.

▶ **Set up the interview.** Interviews can be arranged by telephone, letter, or e-mail. If you make contact with a letter or e-mail, follow up with a telephone call. Indicate in the written correspondence that you will be following up on a specific date and be sure to do so. Include the following information in your request for an informational interview:

- If making contact by telephone, ask whether this is a good time to talk. If not, arrange a better time.
- Provide your name and a brief introduction.
- Give the name of the referring person or state how you found the individual.
- Present your request for a meeting and a brief description of what you hope to accomplish.
- Provide information regarding the follow-up telephone call if you are writing a letter.

▶ **Prepare effectively.** Research the organization as thoroughly as possible. Being knowledgeable demonstrates a genuine interest and increases your credibility. Bring your current resumé. A general resumé may be more effective so that you can revise it based on the outcome of the informational interview. Prepare the questions that you will ask at the interview. Try to ask questions that will help you to gain an understanding of what the job is really like.

▶ **Dress appropriately.** Although less formal than a job interview, the informational interview requires that you present yourself professionally. Chapter 6 discusses professional dressing in depth.

▶ **Pay attention to timeframes.** Typically, informational interviews last 20 to 30 minutes. As with any professional appointment, it is imperative that you arrive on time and respect the time limitations you or your interviewee have set. Effective preparation will allow you to maximize your interview time by having prepared and focused questions.

▶ **Write a thank-you note.** Follow up with a handwritten note expressing your appreciation for the time that the individual spent with you. The note can be brief; it might include appreciation for the time and advice you received along with a summary of the most helpful information. Send the thank-you note within a day or two of the interview.

success steps for informational interviews

- Do your research.
- Select a person to interview.
- Set up the interview.
- Prepare effectively.
- Dress appropriately.
- Pay attention to timeframes.
- Write a thank-you note.

apply it

Informational Interview Preparation

GOAL: To prepare for an effective informational interview

STEP 1: Prepare a list of individuals in your field whom you would like to interview. Consider those who are employed at an organization in which you are interested. Prepare a brief introduction of yourself and your goal.

STEP 2: Prepare a list of topic-related, open-ended questions that would be appropriately asked during an informational interview. Research "informational interview" on the Internet and look for examples of questions that you might use in your interview.

STEP 3: Practice your interview with a classmate, instructor, or other colleague. Ask these people to critique your performance; set goals to improve based on their feedback.

apply it

Informational Interview Practice

GOAL: To prepare for an effective informational interview

STEP 1: Prepare a list of individuals in your field whom you would like to interview. Consider those who can offer information about a job in which you are truly interested.

STEP 2: Prepare a list of questions that you would like to ask each individual. Meet with a group of students who are completing this activity and share ideas for effective interviewing questions.

STEP 3: Team up as pairs and practice your informational interviewing skills. Consider making the practice as realistic as possible by dressing professionally and writing a thank-you note.

STEP 4: Throughout the process, provide constructive feedback and suggestions to your interviewing partner.

JOB FAIRS

Job fairs represent another well-established networking technique. While there are many types of job fairs geared to different audiences, all job fairs seek the same result—to interview as many candidates as possible in one place during a prescribed period of time.

As someone who is just entering the job market in earnest, attending job fairs should be just one of the strategies that you employ during your search. The advantages of job fairs include:

▶ They are generally free to attend.

▶ They are usually local, often hosted by a school or the community.

▶ They bring in several companies to one central location during a set time.

▶ They give you the opportunity to be introduced to industries and positions that you may not have previously considered.

Disadvantages of job fairs include:

▶ The wait in line to speak with a particular recruiter/company can be long.

▶ You may not be able to sell yourself as well as you would like.

▶ The companies with whom you would really like to interview with may not be represented.

In order to maximize your job fair success, consider the following tips, as outlined by Hansen (n.d.[b]).

Before You Go

▶ **Pre-register for the event.** This includes uploading your resumé and any other required information. This will save you time the day of the actual event and gives employers an opportunity to review your resumé prior to an interview. Also be sure to download a list of attending companies and a layout of the venue if available. Most of this information should be online a few days before the start of the job fair.

▶ **Conduct research.** Identify the companies that interest you, and find out as much about them as you can prior to the job fair. Do not wait for company literature that is available that day to hone up on the business.

While You Are There

▶ **Bring plenty of resumés.** Even if you uploaded your resumé during pre-registration, give the recruiter a clean copy. If you have multiple job objectives or interests, bring different versions to the appropriate companies.

▶ **Bring your portfolio.** Even though job fair interviews are typically short, have your professional portfolio with you just in case. You never know when a recruiter will ask to see a sample of your work or a list of references, so be prepared (professional portfolios are covered in Chapter 5 of this textbook).

▶ **Dress appropriately.** You should always wear professional attire to a job fair. Recruiters will be dressed that way, and so should you.

▶ **Have a game plan.** Job fairs are usually very crowded, and moving around can be difficult. Scope out the venue ahead of time, identify the location of the booths of the companies that you want to visit, and prioritize the order in which you want to visit them. Get to the venue prior to the start time so that you have a better chance of being in the front of the line. Just remember to be flexible with your plan as the day goes on.

▶ **Use the quick sell.** Job fair interviews are typically short—often only two to five minutes. Make the most of your time with the interviewer by having an elongated "elevator speech" that can sum up your skills and qualifications and that can express your knowledge of and interest in the company. If you have done your research, you should be able to ask the recruiter specific questions. Above all, remember your interviewing etiquette: have a firm handshake, make eye contact, and be enthusiastic.

▶ **Network.** Your primary task is to network with recruiters, but do not let that stop you from making connections with other attendees and sharing job search strategies and exchanging contact information. Have a good supply of networking business cards with you and hand them out freely (read more about networking business cards later in this chapter). Sometimes employment agencies and a variety of professional organizations also have space set up at job fairs, so make contact there as well.

3

Following Up

▶ **Aftermath.** Just because the job fair is over does not mean that your work is done. Send the recruiters with whom you have spoken a letter thanking them for their time, reiterating your interest in the company or position, reminding them of your qualifications, and expressing your desire for a follow-on interview. A surprising number of job fair applicants fail to do this simple step. Do not be one of them.

NETWORKING BUSINESS CARDS

The rule of thumb when job searching is to always have a stack of resumés with you at all times. But what if handing them out at social or business functions is not practical or advisable?

The answer lies in having networking business cards. Designed to be the same size and shape as traditional business cards, networking cards fill the gap between handing out your resumé or writing your contact information on a cocktail napkin.

Generally, networking cards offer the same contact information as traditional business cards, minus a job title and company name. What differentiates them from business cards is the addition of information about you as an individual, anything from a career focus statement, to a list of accomplishments, to your skill set.

Networking business cards are especially helpful to people just entering the workforce and for those seeking a career change. They can be designed any way you wish, but it is important for the cards to maintain a professional appearance.

Having your "elevator speech" prepared and practiced will allow you to create interest in your abilities and provide opportunities for networking in many places.

Ryan McVay/Getty images

CHAPTER SUMMARY

Networking as a means of developing professional contacts was the main theme of this chapter. You learned what traditional networking is as well as what it is not, and you explored formal and informal networking techniques. Etiquette and follow-up were stressed as important components of the traditional networking process. You also learned about the advent of social networking and personal branding as additional opportunities to aid in your job search. Variations on networking such as elevator speeches, informational interviews, job fairs, and networking business cards were also emphasized.

POINTS TO KEEP IN MIND

In this chapter, several main points were discussed in detail:

▶ Traditional networking is the establishment and maintenance of mutually supportive professional relationships over time.

▶ Networking is *not* getting a referral every time you speak to someone.

▶ Successful networking depends on long-term relationships and giving back to others.

▶ Networking can serve a variety of purposes, although as a college student your main purpose for networking is likely to be finding employment.

▶ Networking opportunities are typically of two types: those that exist and those that you create.

▶ It is critical to write thank-you notes and express appreciation for assistance.

▶ Social networking is an online opportunity to make connections and to showcase your talents and skills as you job search.

▶ Personal branding represents an opportunity to uniquely identify yourself to prospective employers.

▶ Other networking techniques include the elevator speech, the informational interview, job fairs, and networking business cards.

CHECK YOUR UNDERSTANDING

 Visit www.cengagebrain.com to see how well you have mastered the material in Chapter 3.

SUGGESTED ITEMS FOR LEARNING PORTFOLIO

▶ Reflection and Critical Thinking Questions: Include your written responses to these questions. Use them to review your development over time.

▶ Networking Plan: This activity will guide you in developing skills for successful networking.

▌ Networking Preparation: Record the outcomes of this activity in your portfolio and update this resource for your networking events and activities as you develop additional questions and gather information.

▌ Networking Simulation: Keep notes from these practice sessions to help you develop your networking skills.

▌ Elevator Speech Preparation: Record ideas for your elevator speech. As you use them, keep notes regarding their effectiveness.

3

REFERENCES

Bguides.com. (2005). The 9 essentials of networking with people and creating more opportunity (2/e). Guides to get business done™. Richmond, VA. Retrieved February 26, 2013, from http://sandyschwan.typepad.com/sandy_schwan_/files/bguide_professional_networking.pdf

Bryan, E. C. (n.d.). Five strategies for leveraging your online social networks. Retrieved February 26, 2013, from http://www.quintcareers.com/leveraging_social_networks.html

The Career Center at Florida State University. (2007). Conducting an information interview. Retrieved March 5, 2013, from http://www.career.fsu.edu/experience/information-interviews-guide.html

Crosby, O. (2002, Summer). Informational interviewing: Get the inside scoop on careers [Electronic version]. *Occupational Outlook Quarterly, 46*(2). Bureau of Labor and Statistics. Retrieved March 5, 2013, from http://www.bls.gov/opub/ooq/2002/summer/art03.pdf

Donlin, K. (n.d.). Job search expert Kevin Donlin gives career advice. Retrieved February 26, 2013, from http://dev.csp.msu.edu/news/job-search-expert-kevin-donlin-gives-career-advice

Flantzer, H. (n.d.). Networking for career success. Networking for Professionals: The Best in Professional Networking. Retrieved February 26, 2013, from http://networkingforprofessionals.com/art_02.php

Guiseppi, M. (2012). 10 reasons to love your personal brand. Retrieved March 1, 2013, from http://www.quintcareers.com/love_personal_brand.html

Guiseppi, M. (2010). 10 steps to an authentic, magnetic personal brand. Retrieved March 1, 2013, from http://executivecareerbrand.com/10-steps-to-an-authentic-magnetic-personal-brand/

Hansen, R. (n.d.[a]). Building your personal brand: tactics for successful career branding. Retrieved March 1, 2013, from http://www.quintcareers.com /career_branding.html

Hansen, R. (n.d.[b]). The ten keys to success at job and career fairs. Retrieved March 1, 2013, from http://www.quintcareers.com/job _career_fairs.html

Jobvite. (2012[a]). 2012 Social Job Seeker Survey. Retrieved February 27, 2013, from http://web.jobvite.com/121008_JobSeekerSurvey.html

Jobvite. (2012[b]). 2012 Social Recruiting Survey. Retrieved February 22, 2013, from http://recruiting.jobvite.com/resources/social-recruiting -reports-and-trends/

Kovar, R. (n.d.[a]). Networking—A key factor in a successful job search. Networking for Professionals: The Best in Professional Networking. Retrieved February 26, 2013, from http://ezinearticles .com/?Networking—A-Key-Factor-in-a-Successful-Job-Search&id=42128

Kovar, R. (n.d.[b]). People know people. Networking for Professionals: The Best in Professional Networking. Retrieved February 26, 2013, from http://www.networkingforprofessionals.com/search .php?showarticle=12

Kurow, D. (2010). Preparing your elevator speech. Networking for Professionals: The Best in Professional Networking. Retrieved February 26, 2013, from http://dalekurow.com/kurow/preparing-your -elevator-speech

Rangwala, S. (n.d.). Networking 101: Build relationships and advance your career. Retrieved February 26, 2013, from http://www .washingtonpost.com/wp-srv/jobs/how-to/networking-story.html

Schulzke, M. (2010). 5 ways to stay in touch with your extended network. Retrieved February 26, 2013, from http://www.careerrocketeer.com /2010/07/5-ways-to-stay-in-touch-with-your.html

Webopedia. (2010a). Definition of social network. Retrieved February 26, 2013, from http://www.webopedia.com/TERM/S/social_network.html

Webopedia. (2010b). Definition of social networking site. Retrieved February 26, 2013, from http://www.webopedia.com/TERM /S/social_networking_ site.html

CHAPTER OUTLINE

Purpose of the Resumé

Types of Resumés

Resumé Formats

Guidelines to Creating
a Resumé

Strategies for Using
E-Resumés

Cover Letters

Other Types of
Correspondence

References and
Recommendations

Resumé and Cover Letter Development

LEARNING OBJECTIVES

By the end of this chapter, you will achieve the following objectives:

- ▶ Explain the purpose of a resumé.
- ▶ List the elements that are typically required on a resumé.
- ▶ Discuss some general guidelines for preparing a resumé.
- ▶ Compare and contrast the various types of resumés.
- ▶ Describe the various formats in which resumés can be prepared.
- ▶ Explain the general guidelines for making a resumé scannable.
- ▶ Discuss how to appropriately e-mail a resumé.
- ▶ Explain how resumés can be entered into Web databases.
- ▶ Describe how to be cyber-safe.
- ▶ Demonstrate the ability to write a variety of types of correspondence letters.
- ▶ Demonstrate the ability to prepare a professional resumé.
- ▶ Demonstrate the ability to prepare a reference sheet.
- ▶ Demonstrate the ability to write a cover letter.

4

BE IN THE KNOW

And ... Action!

When writing your resumé or cover letter, use action verbs and phrases to describe your accomplishments and skills. Boston College's Career Center (2010) suggests the following list of action verbs that are appropriate to use.

Management Skills	Communication Skills	Clerical or Detailed Skills
administered	addressed	approved
analyzed	arbitrated	arranged
assigned	arranged	catalogued
attained	authored	classified
chaired	corresponded	collected
consolidated	developed	compiled
contracted	directed	dispatched
coordinated	drafted	executed
delegated	edited	generated
developed	enlisted	implemented
directed	formulated	inspected
evaluated	influenced	monitored
executed	interpreted	operated
improved	lectured	organized
increased	mediated	prepared
organized	moderated	processed
oversaw	motivated	purchased
planned	negotiated	recorded
prioritized	persuaded	retrieved
produced	promoted	screened
recommended	publicized	specified
reviewed	reconciled	systematized
scheduled	recruited	tabulated
strengthened	spoke	validated
supervised	translated	
	wrote	

Research Skills	Technical Skills	Teaching Skills
clarified	assembled	adapted
collected	built	advised
critiqued	calculated	clarified
diagnosed	computed	coached
evaluated	designed	communicated
examined	devised	coordinated
extracted	engineered	developed
identified	fabricated	enabled
inspected	maintained	encouraged
interpreted	operated	evaluated
interviewed	overhauled	explained
investigated	programmed	facilitated
organized	remodeled	guided
reviewed	repair	informed
summarized	solved	initiated
surveyed	trained	instructed
systematized	upgraded	persuaded
		set goals
		stimulated

Financial Skills	Creative Skills	Helping Skills
administered	acted	assessed
allocated	conceptualized	assisted
analyzed	created	clarified
appraised	designed	coached
audited	developed	counseled
balanced	directed	demonstrated
budgeted	established	diagnosed
calculated	fashioned	educated
computed	founded	expedited
developed	illustrated	facilitated
forecasted	instituted	familiarized

continued

4

continued

managed	integrated	guided
marketed	introduced	referred
planned	invented	rehabilitated
projected	originated	represented
researched	performed	
	planned	
	revitalized	
	shaped	

PURPOSE OF THE RESUMÉ

The purpose of a resumé is to demonstrate to the reader that you are qualified or have the appropriate skills for a position. The goal of submitting a resumé is to lead to an interview. Because employers have many responsibilities and limited time, applicants need to understand that resumés must say a lot in a very short and concise manner. Typically, an employer will spend no more than 30 seconds reviewing a resumé. Within those 30 seconds, resumés can be either thrown aside or kept for further review.

The resumé should be a statement summarizing your abilities, skills, and professionalism. The words and appearance provide the employer with a first impression of the applicant.

The National Association of Colleges and Employers (n.d.[a]) suggests the following general guidelines for preparing a resumé:

▶ **Own your resumé.** You might find it a daunting task to sit down and put your life on paper, but you are the best person for the job. Seek help and advice from your school's career center or a trusted friend as you fine-tune your resumé.

▶ **Play the "Match Game."** Hiring managers get inundated with resumes with every job they post. The key to getting that coveted interview is to match your skills and abilities with what the employer is seeking. Researching the company and having a full understanding of the job description will help in this regard. The more closely you can make your resumé align with the needs of the organization, the more likely you will be called for an interview.

a.collectionRF/Getty Images

Employers may receive hundreds of resumés for one position and will spend a minimal amount of time reviewing each. Make sure your resumé is professional in its appearance and conveys your skills and abilities at a glance.

▌ **Make your work experience work for you.** Many recent graduates have little to no work experience, and if they do, it may not be a great fit with what a company is looking for. If you completed an internship or did volunteer work that relates directly to the job, be sure to play that up on not only your resumé, but in your cover letter as well (see more about cover letters later in this chapter).

▌ **Attributes are key.** Your transferable skills, such as teamwork, communication skills, initiative, problem solving, and the like are of great value to employers. Make sure that those qualities shine through on your resumé as a differentiator between you and other candidates.

▌ **Don't play hide-and-seek on your resumé**. A well-formatted resumé that is easy to read is the cornerstone for getting you an interview. Employers want facts and relevancy when evaluating a candidate for the job position, so make your wording clear, concise, and valid. No one wants to wade through unnecessary jargon.

▌ **Proof positive.** It goes without saying that you should (and hopefully have others) proof your resumé for spelling and grammatical errors. A surprising number of resumés are sent out with mistakes such as these. This is a red-flag warning that sends a message to prospective employers that you do not care about the company or the position.

▌ **Truth be told.** Embellishment or falsification of your work experience, qualifications, education, or skill set is a recipe for disaster. It may get you the job in the near term, but ultimately there will be consequences in the long term. It is far better to show that you have room to grow in a position than to say you "have it all" and then fail to prove it.

SELF-ASSESSMENT QUESTIONS

- How thorough is your knowledge regarding preparation of a resumé?
- What else would you like to learn about the process of resumé writing?

CRITICAL THINKING QUESTION

▌ How can you determine whether a resumé contains enough material, too much, or too little?

success steps for preparing to write a resumé

- Own your resumé.
- Play the "Match Game."
- Make your work experience work for you.
- Attributes are key.

continued

continued

- Don't play hide-and-seek on your resumé.
- Proof positive.
- Truth be told.

TYPES OF RESUMES

There are a variety of different resumés from which individuals can choose, including these:

- ▶ Chronological resumé
- ▶ Functional resumé
- ▶ Combination resumé (chrono-functional)
- ▶ Curriculum vitae (CV)

The choice of resumé type depends on the applicant's experience and the amount of information the employer is seeking.

THE CHRONOLOGICAL RESUMÉ

The chronological resumé lists professional experience in reverse chronological order. Chronological resumés are typically preferred by employers because they are perceived as fact based and can be easily reviewed. Due to its format, the chronological resumé works best for individuals with "solid experience and a logical job history" (JobStar Central, 2006a). Those who have experienced career changes and lack experience may find the chronological resumé more difficult to use. Figure 4-1 is an example of the chronological resumé.

THE FUNCTIONAL RESUMÉ

The functional resumé lists experience by type rather than chronologically. For example, on a functional resumé, management experience from several positions would be grouped in one section. Computer skills would be grouped in another. Some employers may feel that the functional resumé is more difficult to review, as it is less structured

Resumé Sample: Chronological Format

Seth Robertson
23 First Street ■ Albany, NY 12208
(518) 555-3647 ■ srobertson@gmail.com

WORK EXPERIENCE:

September 2013 to Present   Assistant Bookkeeper, Achievement Office Sales/Service, Albany, NY. Aid in
                             bookkeeping, payroll services, and tax preparation.

September 2012 to May 2013   Internship at Goldworthy & Ames Certified Public Accountants, Albany,
                             NY. Provided tax preparation assistance for five major clients.

September 2010 to April 2011 Tutor, Teaching and Learning Center, The College of Saint Rose, Albany, NY. Provided
                             tutoring assistance in Math 121, 122 and Statistics I and II to students on an individual
                             basis.

May 2000 to September 2004   Groundskeeper, Albany High School, Albany, NY. Maintained school grounds during
                             summer break.

EDUCATION:

September 2009 to May 2013   The College of Saint Rose, Albany, NY
                             Bachelor of Science degree in Business Administration conferred in May 2004
                             Accounting GPA: 3.8
                             Overall GPA: 3.5

COMPUTER SKILLS: Microsoft Office and Apple applications

LEADERSHIP EXPERIENCES: Supervisor and team leader of client audits. Co-captain 2008–2009 State Championship
                             basketball team. Two gold medals and one bronze–Team Handball–Empire State Games

REFERENCES: Available upon request.

Figure 4-1   A chronological resumé lists the applicant's experience in the order in which it occurred.

than a chronological resumé and it is more difficult to associate experience with a specific job.

JobStar Central (2006b) states that the functional resumé works best for those individuals

- whose work history is varied, with no clear career link between each job.
- who are new college graduates entering the workforce with little work experience.
- whose past job titles do not clearly indicate the level of skills used.
- who are trying to make a career change.

Figure 4-2 illustrates the functional resumé.

Resumé Sample: Functional Format

Seth Robertson
23 First Street ■ Albany, NY 12208
(518) 555-3647 ■ srobertson@gmail.com

SKILLS/ACHIEVEMENTS: Supervisor and team leader of client audits.
Excellent computer skills, including Microsoft Office and Apple applications.
Working with clients and interpreting their needs.
Working under the pressure of deadlines.

EMPLOYMENT HISTORY: Assistant Bookkeeper, Achievement Office Sales/Service, Albany, NY. 2013 to present.
Intern, Goldworthy & Ames Certified Public Accountants, Albany, NY. 2012 to 2013.
Tutor, Teaching and Learning Center, The College of Saint Rose, Albany, NY. 2010 to 2011.
Groundskeeper, Albany High School, Albany, NY. 2009 to 2013.

EDUCATION: Bachelor of Science degree, Business Administration, The College of Saint Rose,
Albany, NY. May 2013.

RELEVANT COURSES: Financial Accounting, Behavioral Science in Business, Urban Economics, Managerial Economics,
Financial Information Systems, Taxation, Strategic Marketing Planning, Investment Theory,
New Business Ventures and the Entrepreneur, Performance and Financial Auditing.

REFERENCES: Available upon request.

Figure 4-2   A functional resumé presents the applicant's experience by type.

COMBINATION RESUMÉS

Sometimes referred to as a chrono-functional resumé, a combination resumé blends features of both chronological and functional resumés. Figure 4-3 is an example of a combination resumé.

THE CURRICULUM VITAE

Depending on the profession, the curriculum vitae may be most appropriate. The curriculum vitae (CV) is a detailed description of all academic and professional pursuits, including educational endeavors, professional positions and their related duties, publications, presentations given and attended, volunteer work, organizational memberships and positions held, and honors and recognition that have been received. Although the chronological or functional resumé is no more than one or two pages, a curriculum vitae can be 15 to 20 pages. The CV is most commonly used in academic and research settings. The detail of a CV makes it appropriate mainly for individuals who have extensive experience and credentials.

Resumé Sample: Combination Format

Seth Robertson
23 First Street ■ Albany, NY 12208
(518) 555-3647 ■ srobertson@gmail.com

SKILLS/ACHIEVEMENTS:	Supervisor and team leader of client audits. Excellent computer skills, including Microsoft Office and Apple applications. Working with clients and interpreting their needs. Working under the pressure of deadlines.
WORK EXPERIENCE:	
September 2013 to Present	Assistant Bookkeeper, Achievement Office Sales/Service, Albany, NY. Aid in bookkeeping, payroll services, and tax preparation.
September 2012 to May 2013	Internship at Goldworthy & Ames Certified Public Accountants, Albany, NY. Provided tax preparation assistance for five major clients.
September 2010 to April 2011	Tutor, Teaching and Learning Center, The College of Saint Rose, Albany, NY. Provided tutoring assistance in Math 121, 122 and Statistics I and II to students on an individual basis.
May 2000 to September 2004	Groundskeeper, Albany High School, Albany, NY. Maintained school grounds during summer break.
EDUCATION:	
September 2009 to May 2013	The College of Saint Rose, Albany, NY Bachelor of Science degree in Business Administration conferred in May 2004 Accounting GPA: 3.8 Overall GPA: 3.5
REFERENCES:	Available upon request.

Figure 4-3 A combination resumé uses features of both the chronological and functional resumés.

RESUMÉ FORMATS

Resumé formats will depend on your field and the requirements of the employer. Consider the following formats.

ELECTRONIC RESUMÉS

An electronic resumé is intended to be delivered via e-mail or through an online application form. The electronic resumé has no text formatting, making it scannable, or able to be read by any e-mail or resumé database or tracking program. For example, using all capital letters in a standard font such as Times or Helvetica for headings eliminates formatting that might be specific to your word processing program.

Self-Assessment Questions

- With which of the resumé formats are you familiar? With which would you like to become more familiar?
- If you have an existing resumé, how do you think your chosen format has served you in the past? If it has been effective, why? If not, why not?

4

The following guidelines to facilitate electronic processing of a resumé are suggested by R. S. Hansen (n.d.):

- Use one of the standard serif or sans serif typefaces, such as Courier, Times, Helvetica, Futura, Arial, Optima, Palatino, Univers. Avoid using decorative fonts.

- Use a normal type size, usually in the range of 11 to 14 points. The maximum number of characters per line is 65 (partly dependent on type size).

- Avoid any kinds of graphics or shading.

- Keep formatting simple. Use all caps for major headings, but avoid bolding, italicizing, and underlining.

- Do not use bullets or lines.

- Left-justify text.

- If your resumé is more than one page, place your name at the top of each additional page.

WEB RESUMÉS

A Web resumé is posted on the Internet and is typically used to display an individual's skills in designing hypertext markup language (HTML) documents. A Web resumé is beneficial to individuals seeking art or graphics positions and can include electronic media such as video, audio, and advanced graphics.

SELECTING A RESUMÉ FORMAT

Experts recommend keeping copies of your resumé in various formats so that you will be prepared to respond to a specific employer's request. Dikel (2010) recommends the following formats:

- A printable version completed in a word processing program that can be printed and mailed in hard copy. A printable version of your resumé can include elements such as boldface type, bullets, and graphics. You will want to have a professional hard copy of your resumé to hand to a hiring manager during an interview.

- A scannable version that has less design elements than a printable version. Bulleted lists work in this version, but that is about the upper end of the design spectrum. Scannable resumés are less in vogue now because e-mailed resumés can be put directly into resumé databases (Hansen & Hansen, n.d.).

- A plaintext (ASCII) version appropriate for pasting into online forms. This version follows the guidelines for an electronic resumé.

- An e-mail version (also ASCII) that is formatted for the length-of-line restrictions in e-mail and meets the requirements for an electronic resumé.

Another version that is gaining wider acceptance is a resumé designed as a portable document format (pdf). The best thing about pdf files is that they are compatible with many different platforms and they do not lose any formatting. One drawback is that they are difficult to put into resumé databases (Hansen & Hansen, n.d.).

? CRITICAL THINKING QUESTION

- What is your reaction to the following statement? "Because it takes a lot of extra work to create various versions of the resumé, I don't think that is necessary."

4

CASE IN POINT: FOR APPEARANCE SAKE

Read the scenario below. Then, in groups or as a class, discuss the questions at the end.

As a college graduate, Mike Lanham has become very successful in his profession. In his newly acquired position as a manager, Mike's first task is to hire individuals to fill a number of vacant positions within his department. This will be Mike's first experience in hiring. The positions Mike must fill range from highly technical to clerical. To begin the process of hiring, Mike reviews the received resumés. In addition to the technical skills and abilities that are listed, Mike also pays close attention to the appearance of the resumé. From the appearance, Mike believes he can more easily identify organized individuals.

- How can a resumé indicate whether an individual is organized, detailed, and professional?

- How much weight should the appearance of a resumé carry in the selection process?

- Do you think Mike is being unfair to applicants who do not exhibit these skills through the appearance of their resumés? Should Mike consider these individuals anyway?

- If you have developed a resumé, do you think your resumé indicates that you are an organized, detailed, and professional individual? If so, how? If not, why not?

GUIDELINES TO CREATING A RESUMÉ

Regardless of the resumé format, employers typically need similar information. Include the following information on the resumé, not necessarily in this order (Hess, 2007):

▶ Contact information, including name, address, telephone number, and e-mail address

▶ Summary of qualifications

▶ Education, including names and locations of schools, dates attended and date of graduation, major course of study, and degree earned

▶ Work history (paid experience)

▶ Volunteer work history (unpaid experience)

▶ Specialty certifications, credentials, or licenses

▶ Military experience

▶ Professional memberships and positions held

▶ Information regarding special skills, recognition, and achievements

The following are some simple guidelines to follow when compiling your resumé:

▶ **Customize your resumé.** A resumé targeted at a specific job is most effective. Customize your resumé so that your skills and achievements support the job for which you are applying. This does mean that you will need to adjust your resumé each time you apply for a job, but better results are worth that extra effort.

▶ **Be prepared with the information you need to write your resumé.** Collect all pertinent information such as job history, transcripts, certifications, and other documents that contain data that you will include on your resumé. This eliminates or minimizes the need to search for information and will make more efficient use of your time.

▶ **Select the best resumé type for your needs.** Be clear on which resumé type is the best choice for effectively presenting your information relative to the job requirements. Make sure to check on whether an electronic resumé is required.

▶ **Use available resources to help with the composition of your resumé.** There are a variety of resources that provide sample copies and suggestions for resumés. Conduct an Internet search using "resumés" or "resumé writing" as your search term. Also, seek assistance from the career center on your campus.

▶ **Consider additions to your resumé based on your field.** Depending on the job for which you are applying, additions to the resumé can be helpful. For example, in the graphic arts field, added visual interest can demonstrate creativity. Follow the standards of your field. Whatever you add should be simple and professional. Your words should be the focus.

▶ **Limit the length of functional or chronological resumés.** A length of one or two pages is ideal. Pages should be added only if they are absolutely necessary to effectively represent your experience.

▶ **Use bullets for an easy read.** Avoid using long sentences and being too wordy. Use phrases that convey your points clearly and concisely.

▶ **Use action verbs and phrases to describe your accomplishments and skills.** Select words that convey precise and efficient action when describing your accomplishments. According to Barthel and Goldrick-Jones (n.d., "Consider Word Choice Carefully"), your resumé should "sound positive and confident; neither too aggressive nor overly modest." Examples of action verbs include *created, modified, directed, supervised, wrote, illustrated,* and *managed.*

▶ **Use a professional tone.** Avoid extensive use of pronouns such as "I" or "me," especially at the beginning of paragraphs. Write in a formal conversational tone. Avoid contractions (use "do not" instead of "don't") and avoid abbreviations and slang.

▶ **Use a professional e-mail address.** E-mail addresses that are used socially, intended to be fun and amusing, may not be appropriate for professional correspondence. Thoughtfully consider your e-mail address. If it in any way presents an unprofessional image or can be interpreted as offensive, consider creating another account for professional use. Your Internet service provider (ISP) may offer additional mailboxes with your subscription or you may use one of the free services

? CRITICAL THINKING QUESTIONS

▶ What other action verbs can you think of? Compile a list and refer to it when writing your resumé.

▶ Which action verbs are most appropriate for your field and experience?

4

4

offered on the Internet. A professional e-mail would be your name or a variation on it. An example is susan.smith @yourISP.com.

▶ **Include all important information that employers will want.** For example, a job history must include the name of the employer, your job title, job location, and dates of employment. Reasons for leaving a job should not be included.

▶ **Check for accuracy.** Make sure your address, phone numbers, and e-mail address are correct. Use only permanent addresses. Ensure that your outgoing voice mail message is professional and appropriate for an employer to hear.

▶ **Represent well-rounded skills.** Include both technical and soft skills on your resumé.

▶ **Use discretion with personal interests.** Personal hobbies and activities should not be listed unless they are related to the job you are seeking.

▶ **Be honest about your abilities.** Never embellish your experience or skills. You do not want to mislead employers to assume you are more qualified than you actually are.

▶ **Include only postsecondary experience.** As a college graduate, list only your college experience. High school graduation should not be listed.

▶ **Do not list personal information on your resumé.** Information pertaining to religion, marital status, and ethnicity should not be listed on the resumé.

▶ **Limit lengthy experience.** If your work experience spans more than 10 years, it is acceptable to list the most recent 10 years only. List more only if the experience relates directly to the job.

▶ **Pay attention to mechanics.** Make sure your resumé is professional by paying close attention to spacing, spelling, and grammar. Barthel and Goldrick-Jones (n.d., "Evaluate Your Resumé") suggest that you assess the appearance of your resumé and ask the following questions:

• Is the page too busy with different type styles, sizes, lines, or boxes?

- Is there too much white space? (White space is the area on the resumé that does not contain any writing or graphics.) White space should be sufficient to allow easy reading, but not so much that the content appears sparse.
- Is important information quick and easy to find?

▶ **Get a professional opinion.** Ask a professional, such as the personnel in your campus career center or a colleague in the field, to review your resumé. Be open to constructive criticism. You want your resumé to be the best it can be.

▶ **Include a thoughtful career objective.** Include a career objective that is stated as a goal and reflects the characteristics of the position you are seeking. An example of a career objective is "Seeking a position as a medical assistant in a medium-size family practice." The career objective is placed at the beginning of the resumé, following your contact information.

▶ **Check for legibility.** If providing a hard copy to the employer, make sure the printed copy of your resumé is easy to read and that the paper is of good quality. High-quality white paper is the most appropriate.

▶ **List references separately.** Speak to people who know you and your work about being a reference for you. List them on a separate reference sheet.

success steps for completing a resumé

- Be prepared with the information you need prior to writing your resumé.
- Select the best resumé type for your needs.
- Use resources on the Internet to help with the composition of your resumé.
- Consider additions to your resumé based on your field.
- Try to limit functional or chronological resumés to one page.
- Use bullets for an easy read.
- Use action verbs and phrases to describe your accomplishments and skills.

continued

SELF-ASSESSMENT QUESTIONS

- What did you learn from the resumé guidelines?
- If you have an existing resumé, how might your resumé change based on what you have learned from the guidelines?

CRITICAL THINKING QUESTION

▶ Do you think it is important to follow these guidelines, or do you think more individuality should be allowed when it comes to content and style on one's resumé?

4

continued

- Use a professional tone.
- Don't leave out important information that employers will want.
- Check for accuracy.
- Represent well-rounded skills.
- Use discretion about including personal interests.
- Be honest about your abilities.
- Include only postsecondary experience.
- Do not list personal information on your resumé.
- Limit lengthy experience.
- Pay attention to mechanics.
- Check for legibility.
- List references separately.

STRATEGIES FOR USING E-RESUMÉS

Any more, companies prefer that candidates apply online through company web sites or Internet job boards. It is more efficient, convenient, and cost-effective to conduct job searches in this manner. K. Hansen (n.d.[b]) lists strategies that are critical for creating an effective resumé that will get into the hands of a prospective employer:

- **An electronic resumé is a MUST.** There is no getting around today's technology and delivery systems for posting and sending your resumé. "More than 80 percent of employers are now placing resumés directly into searchable databases and an equal percentage of employers prefer to receive resumés by e-mail," states Hansen.

- **Keywords are key.** Resumé databases have search capabilities based on keywords. Employers look for those keywords within the body of your resumé to see whether your qualifications match the job description. If your resumé does not contain searchable keywords, then you are basically out of luck. Take the time to tailor your resumé and cover letter to match keywords listed on the job posting.

Today, resumés are commonly sent via e-mail or posted on the Internet. Remember that in some situations, however, it is a good practice to also send a hard copy via surface mail.

Echo/Cultura/Getty Images

▶ **Your e-resumé must be filled with accomplishments.** Accomplishments stand out much more than job duties on a resumé, electronic or not. This ties back in to the use of keywords and how you can direct the employer to what you have achieved in your job, and not merely just what you do in your job.

▶ **Read the instructions so you post your resumé according to the requirements of the employer or job board.** Some want the resumé sent as an attachment, others want it embedded within the body of an e-mail, and others want it submitted into an online form.

The National Association of Colleges and Employers (n.d.[b]) offers these additional tips for making an electronic application outstanding:

▶ Follow directions on the application. Make sure you are entering data into the correct fields.

▶ Complete all fields, even those that employers do not require.

▶ Make sure that your career objective is strong. It should identify what skills you bring to the job, not what kind of job you are hoping to get.

▶ If an optional assessment test is offered online, be sure to take it. Some companies will automatically reject your application if you fail to complete the test.

▶ Use the comments section wisely. Here you can complete a skills inventory or show that you have completed research on the company or the industry.

▶ Use a spelling and grammar check if that option is available. If not, double- and triple-check your application before hitting the "Submit" button.

▶ Cover letters and resumés are excellent places to use quotes from recommendation letters. Again, think of keywords that will pop out at an employer.

SAFETY ON THE WEB

With the growing use of Internet technologies, individuals need to take some precautions to remain cyber-safe when posting their resumés or other personal information. Resumeminers (2007) gives this advice:

▶ **Identity theft remains a huge issue.** Resumés are an excellent place for thieves to extract personal information about you. Remove normal contact information and your business

4

and personal e-mail addresses, and go with a generic e-mail account (such as jobsearcher@hotmail.com). Also, employers sometimes search resumé posting boards looking for current employees. Don't let them find you!

▶ **Beware of fraud.** If contacted by a company via e-mail or phone, do not give out your Social Security number, bank account information, or credit card numbers.

▶ **Do not use your employer's assets to job search.** Employers have successfully won court cases where a current employee used computers, telephones, and Internet connections to job search. Find new employment on your own time and on your own equipment.

The following are some safety considerations recommended by Dikel (2010):

▶ **Limit where you post your resumé on the Internet.** Avoid "overposting." Limit your postings to three or four job sites.

▶ **Pay attention to privacy policies.** Ensure that your personal information will not be released without your knowledge.

▶ **Expect a trial period.** Use sites that allow you to view and evaluate the usefulness of the site before making a long-term commitment.

▶ **Give general information.** Use general information and descriptions to present employment history. Avoid using company names and dates of employment.

▶ **Keep information current.** Repost your resumé every 14 days so that it appears as a fresh submission. If a response is not received in a month or so, remove it and find another posting site.

▶ **Remove promptly when appropriate.** Once you are hired, delete all posted resumés.

SELF-ASSESSMENT QUESTION

• What concerns might you have regarding the use of some of these more advanced methods for sending your resumé? What might you do to overcome these concerns?

? CRITICAL THINKING QUESTION

▶ How might technology continue to change how resumés are sent to employers?

success steps for being cyber-safe

• Watch out for identity theft.
• Beware of fraud.
• Job search on your own time and with your own equipment.

- Limit where you post your resumé on the Internet.
- Pay attention to privacy policies.
- Expect a trial period.
- Give general information.
- Keep information current.
- Remove your resumé promptly when appropriate.

apply it

Utilizing Technology to Send Resumés

GOAL: *To develop a clearer understanding of how to use technology to send resumés*

STEP 1: Conduct research on the Web to further understand how technology can be used to send your resumé.

STEP 2: If technology is not your strength, schedule a meeting with someone who is more knowledgeable in this area to help clarify areas that are unclear.

STEP 3: Write a report of your findings and what you learned.

STEP 4: Consider placing this report in your Learning Portfolio.

COVER LETTERS

The cover letter is a tool for introducing yourself to an employer and is a required element when submitting a resumé. The cover letter provides the opportunity to give additional information regarding your skills and experience and to summarize how they relate to the desired job. The cover letter should clearly convey what you have to offer to the employer. Do not focus on yourself; avoid statements such as "This would be a great opportunity for me." The cover letter should not exceed one page in length. Princeton University Career Services

(2010) provides the following general guidelines to consider when developing a cover letter:

▶ Each cover letter should be written in response to the specific job requirements. Sending a generic cover letter is strongly discouraged.

▶ Keep copies of all cover letters in order to refer back to as needed.

▶ The cover letter must provide information that clearly illustrates how your skills and experiences match what the organization is seeking.

▶ Whenever possible, cover letters should be addressed to a specific person.

▶ If the job comes through a referral, mention this in the cover letter. Include this information in the opening paragraph. A familiar name is more likely to capture and hold the interest of the reader.

▶ Professionalism in the cover letter is as critical as in the resumé. Pay attention to elements such as spelling, grammar, spacing, professional tone, and paper quality. Elements of the cover letter should match those in the resumé.

The cover letter can also provide the prospective employer a glimpse into who the applicant is as an individual.

The Writing Center at Rensselaer Polytechnic Institute (n.d.) recommends that the format of the cover letter include the following:

▶ Paragraphs should reflect a formal conversational tone.

▶ The first paragraph usually is brief and tells which job you are applying for as well as where you learned about the position.

▶ The body of the letter can range from one to three paragraphs. These paragraphs provide the opportunity to elaborate on your qualifications and experiences. Being specific regarding how these abilities and experiences match well with the desired job is critical.

▶ The last paragraph contains a request for further contact and states how this contact can be achieved.

Figure 4-4 shows a sample cover letter.

A well-written cover letter can provide the prospective employer with information about an applicant's personality, ability for being detailed, communication skills, enthusiasm, and intelligence.

Wuka/E+/Getty Images

Kathleen Brooks
432 East Brooks Avenue
Denver, CO 80000

November 3, 2013

Ms. Christina Chung
Human Resources Director
Everett Technologies
10067 Mountain View Road
Broomfield, CO 82222

Dear Ms. Chung:

Enclosed please find my resumé in support of my interest in the office manager position that was advertised in the October 30, 2013 edition of the Denver Gazette and posted on Everett Technologies' Web site.

The experience that I would bring to Everett Technologies includes a background as an assistant office manager, overseeing the streamlining of various office procedures, and implementing data tracking systems. My qualifications effectively support your stated company goal of developing and putting into practice a new client data management system.

I would very much like to discuss ways in which my experience could contribute to a smooth and efficient transition to a new system and would value the opportunity to further explore how I might support your efforts in the office manager position. Thank you for your consideration and I look forward to hearing from you.

Sincerely,

Kathleen Brooks

Figure 4-4   An effective cover letter provides the employers with a concise yet clear overview of your skills and goals.

apply it

Job Search Materials

GOAL: *To demonstrate the ability to develop a resumé, cover letter, and reference sheet*

STEP 1: Use the information from this chapter and other available resources to develop a resumé, cover letter, and reference sheet.

STEP 2: Share your resumé with a respected professional and ask for constructive criticism.

STEP 3: Redo areas as instructed by the reviewer and submit to your instructor for review.

STEP 4: Consider putting this project in your Learning Portfolio.

OTHER TYPES OF CORRESPONDENCE

There are other types of correspondence frequently utilized by the job seeker. You should familiarize yourself with these other types of correspondence as they can aid you in your job search. As with a cover letter, place high regard on professionalism.

▶ **Application Letter.** An application letter is similar to a cover letter in that it is used to introduce a candidate for an advertised and sometimes unadvertised or unsolicited position. Where the two types of letters differ is that an application letter is more detailed in describing the candidate's work history, education, and how he or she would be a qualified fit for the job. Application letters are generally longer in length (perhaps up to four paragraphs) than a cover letter. They are especially useful if the candidate is applying for an academic program on campus or is seeking an internship (Mayhew, n.d.).

▶ **Networking Letter.** As you have learned, networking is a powerful tool that you can use to help you in your job search. In concert with that technique is the use of a networking letter. A networking letter is used as an introduction to someone who you feel could aid you in your job search or career decision, perhaps a college alumnus or a businessperson who came recommended to you. The letter serves as a vehicle to set up an informational interview with that individual to gain insight, advice, or other information. It is not necessary to send a resumé with a networking letter, as you are not requesting a job interview with that individual.

▶ **Prospecting Letter.** A prospecting letter, also known as a letter of inquiry or interest, is used when you know of an organization that may be hiring but has not advertised a specific opening for a position. Your letter should indicate your interest in and understanding of the company, and how your skills and education would be a good fit with the organization. Prospecting letters indicate a desire for an interview and a suggested timeframe for contacting the individual to whom the letter is being sent. Include a copy of your resum**é** with the letter (Doyle, n.d.).

▶ **Career Change Letter.** A career change letter is a type of cover letter designed to fill a particular niche. When you are applying for a position that is not in your current field (and thus is not supported by your work history listed on your resumé), it is of vital importance that you focus on your transferable skills that you can bring to this new position. Hone in on what you have learned at your previous job: communication skills, supervisory or management experience, recognition as a valued team member, and the like. Give focus to your desire to learn new skills (that is why you are changing careers, right?) and your enthusiasm for doing so. The more you can convince the reader of your letter that you will be helping the organization by virtue of your skill set, the greater your chances of landing that coveted interview.

By today's standards, is it better sending these types of letters via regular mail, or via e-mail? Basically, both forms are acceptable, although the company culture can help guide you (K. Hansen, n.d.[a]). An e-mailed thank you is also appropriate if you know that the company will be making a hiring decision quickly. The important point here is that you follow through in a timely manner. As with the cover letter, these letters continue to represent the applicant's professionalism. The same attention given to the cover letter should be given to any of these types of correspondence.

SELF-ASSESSMENT QUESTION

- How effective are your professional letters? Where might you go for help in developing these skills?

? CRITICAL THINKING QUESTION

▶ What is your reaction to the following statement? "A generic cover letter is sufficient, as writing a customized letter for each potential job is too time-consuming."

4

REFERENCES AND RECOMMENDATIONS

Employers usually request the names of individuals who are familiar with your professional performance and will attest to your skills, abilities, and overall professionalism. Include the name, title, address, phone number, and e-mail address of each reference. List the elements of each reference on separate lines, as you would when addressing an envelope. Robinson (n.d.) makes the following suggestions for locating individuals who will consent to being listed as references and provide positive recommendations:

▶ Always ask a person to be a reference. Don't assume that because you know the person professionally she will consent to recommending you. Also take into consideration the amount of time a reference might have to field phone calls from the hiring company. Carefully consider what type of reference you will be given by this person. A neutral recommendation is

4

considered negative. Only seek out those individuals who you know will describe you in positive terms.

▶ Consider who would make a good reference. It should be someone with whom your work (and don't forget volunteer work here) has been closely aligned. Consider supervisors, coworkers, and professors. Family members and friends are not considered professional references.

▶ Make sure your references have the tools they need when the employer contacts them. This includes a current copy of your resumé, the job description, and even background information on the company. Make it as easy as possible for your reference to align your skills and experience with the position.

▶ Keep your references in the loop. Let them know when they might receive a phone call and who will be calling (if that information is available to you). Also let them know the status of the job, such as whether you were offered the position and whether you accepted.

▶ Always thank your references with a personal note. Even if you weren't offered the job or chose not to take it, you may need this person's help again in another job search.

▶ Stay in touch with your references after the fact. Professional social networking or traditional networking techniques are effective ways of staying connected.

▶ Keep your reference list updated as you would your resumé.

apply it

Preparing Professional Correspondence

GOAL: To demonstrate the ability to develop a variety of letters used to correspond during the job search

STEP 1: The instructor will divide the class into two groups. Each group should be given at least three different types of correspondence letters.

STEP 2: Each group conducts research regarding group members' letters and the appropriate content, layout, and purpose of each. The group compiles a short report on these findings and presents it to the class. Handouts or overheads should be encouraged.

STEP 3: Each group member must also write one letter of each type he or she has researched and turn them in to the instructor for review.

STEP 4: Consider putting the correspondence examples from this activity in your Learning Portfolio.

Look for examples of Letters of Recommendation and a Reference List on this textbook's companion web site.

? CRITICAL THINKING QUESTION

▶ What specific questions might you ask an individual whom you are considering using as a reference?

CHAPTER SUMMARY

This chapter provided the foundations for preparing a resumé, cover letter, and other types of professional correspondence used during the job search process. You learned how to select content for each type of correspondence, as well as how to present it professionally and effectively. Various formats for submitting resumés were reviewed, and you received guidelines for selecting the most appropriate format for your needs.

POINTS TO KEEP IN MIND

In this chapter, several main points were discussed in detail:

▶ The purpose of a resumé is to spark an interest with the potential employer by pointing out your abilities, skills, and professionalism.

▶ Resumés must be short, concise, yet full of details.

▶ Resumé types include chronological, functional, combination, and the curriculum vitae.

▶ Recent college graduates typically choose to use either the functional or combination resumé.

▶ Various formats of resumés include printed, scannable, plain-text, e-mail, and Web versions.

▶ Standard guidelines for creating a resumé include using bullets for an easier read, avoiding long sentences and wordiness, and using action verbs and phrases to describe your accomplishments and skills.

▶ Items that you should not use on your resumé include personal pronouns, temporary addresses and phone numbers, and lists of personal hobbies and activities that are unrelated to the job.

▶ Your resumé can be sent to an employer in several ways, ranging from traditional methods such as mailing and faxing, to more contemporary methods such as e-mailing or posting on the Internet.

4

❯ The cover letter, which must always accompany the resumé, should provide further details regarding your skills and experience and how these directly relate to the desired job.

❯ Other types of correspondence you may use include application letters, career change letters, networking letters, and prospecting letters.

❯ References need to be individuals who offer a positive recommendation, present your skills effectively, and exhibit good overall communication skills.

CHECK YOUR UNDERSTANDING

Visit www.cengagebrain.com to see how well you have mastered the material in Chapter 4.

SUGGESTED ITEMS FOR LEARNING PORTFOLIO

❯ Using Technology to Send Resumés: This activity is intended to help you develop a clearer understanding of how to use technology to send resumés.

❯ Job Search Materials: By completing this activity, you will gain experience in developing a resumé, cover letter, and reference sheet.

❯ Preparing Professional Correspondence: The goal of this activity is to provide practice in creating a variety of letters used to correspond during the job search.

REFERENCES

Barthel, B., & Goldrick-Jones, A. (n.d.). Resumés [Electronic version]. The Writing Center at Rensselaer Polytechnic Institute. Retrieved April 22, 2013, from http://www.mil-sat.com/images/resume.html#Consider

Career Center Boston College. (2010). Resume Action Verbs. Retrieved May 10, 2013, from http://www.bc.edu/offices/careers/skills/resumes/verbs.html

Dikel, M. F. (2010). Prepare your resumé for emailing or online posting. Retrieved April 22, 2013, from http://www.rileyguide.com/eresumé.html

Doyle, A. (n.d.). Letter of interest. Retrieved May 2, 2013, from http://jobsearch.about.com/od/coverlettersamples/a/letterinterest.htm

Hansen, K. (n.d.[a]). FAQs about job-seeker thank you letters. Retrieved April 22, 2013, from http://www.quintcareers.com/thank_you_letters.html

Hansen, K. (n.d.[b]). The top 10 things you need to know about e-resumés and posting your resumé online. Retrieved April 22, 2013, from http://www.quintcareers.com/e-resumés.html

Hansen, R. S. (n.d.). How to write job-search text resumés. Retrieved April 22, 2013, from http://www.quintcareers.com/scannable_resumés.html

Hansen, R. S., & Hansen, K. (n.d.). What resumé format is best for you? Retrieved April 22, 2013, from http://www.quintcareers.com/best_resumé_format.html

Hess, P. M. (2007). *Career Success: Right Here Right Now! 2/e* (pp. 80–85). South-Western Educational Publication.

JobStar Central. (2006a). What is the right resumé for me? Chronological. Retrieved April 22, 2013, from http://jobstar.org/tools/resumé/res-chro.php

JobStar Central. (2006b). What is the right resumé for me? Functional. Retrieved April 22, 2013, from http://jobstar.org/tools/resumé/res-func.php

Mayhew, R. (n.d.). Application letter vs. cover letter. Retrieved May 2, 2013, from http://work.chron.com/application-letter-vs-cover-letter-5451.html

National Association of Colleges and Employers. (n.d.[a]). Build the resume employers want. Retrieved April 30, 2013, from http://www.nxtbook.com/nxtbooks/nace/JobChoices0812/index.php#/48

National Association of Colleges and Employers. (n.d.[b]). How to apply online and get an employer's attention. Retrieved April 22, 2013, from http://umaine.edu/career/files/2010/10/How-To-Apply-Online.pdf

Princeton University Career Services. (2010). http://www.princeton.edu/career/pdfs/guide/8_Career-Services-Guide_Cover-Letters-and-E-mail.pdf

Resumeminers. (2007). Safe job hunting. Retrieved April 22, 2013, from http://www.resuméminers.com/Job-Search-Sites/Safe-Job-Hunting.htm

Robinson, K. (n.d.). 10 tips for top-notch references. Retrieved April 22, 2013, from http://www.indianatech.edu/CurrentStudents/CareerCenter/vcc/Documents/10%20Tips%20for%20Top%20Notch%20References.pdf

The Writing Center at Rensselaer Polytechnic Institute. (2009). Cover letters. Retrieved April 22, 2013, from http://www.ccp.rpi.edu/?s=cover+letters&searchbutton=Go%21

4

CHAPTER OUTLINE

Developing a Professional Portfolio

LEARNING OBJECTIVES

By the end of this chapter, you will achieve the following objectives:

▶ Discuss the purpose of developing a professional portfolio.

▶ Describe the different types of portfolios and explain how each fulfills a specific purpose.

▶ Select appropriate artifacts for each of the portfolio types.

▶ Select an organizational strategy appropriate to the type and purpose of the portfolio.

▶ Devise a method of portfolio evaluation.

▶ Assemble the beginnings of a professional portfolio.

BE IN THE KNOW

Thanks for Your Support

In an earlier chapter you learned the significance of personal branding and how having an effective strategy for creating one can help differentiate you from "the pack." Be sure that your personal brand carries over when it comes to creating your portfolio.

One simple way to accomplish this is to peruse portfolio web sites for examples and inspiration. Even if you are not an overly creative person or are not pursuing a career in the arts, you can still tap into the ideas of others. You will want to carry your theme through on all of your marketing materials: your resumé, networking business cards, and your portfolio. Remember, your personal brand should be fluid and subject to updating. Keep your supporting materials that way as well.

5

PURPOSES OF PROFESSIONAL PORTFOLIOS

Imagine an artist who is applying for a job as an illustrator. The artist's resumé lists an impressive array of previous jobs and describes the artist's skills and abilities. His references from previous employers are all excellent. The potential employer, although impressed with the artist's resumé, wants to know that his style fits the illustration criteria of the publisher. The employer looks at the artist's work showcased in his portfolio and makes a decision about the work based on tangible examples.

Internweb.com (n.d.) points out that although portfolios are familiar in fields such as the creative and visual arts, they are not as well known in other fields. Although less commonly utilized in fields outside of the arts, professional portfolios can benefit job seekers in any profession.

The general purpose of the portfolio is to provide examples of work that an individual can perform. Internweb.com (n.d.) summarizes the purpose of a professional portfolio as follows: "A strong professional career portfolio provides direct evidence of your related accomplishments. It provides potential employers with a 'snapshot' of your achievements to date, the type of work you've done, and the type of employee you will be. A professional portfolio goes beyond a cover letter and resumé. Rather than simply telling an employer about your skills, it provides evidence of them."

It should be noted that a professional portfolio is the culmination of several years of academic work you have completed. You should consider starting to accumulate items for your portfolio at the beginning of your academic career. This way, you will have a strong body of work to show prospective employers. Furthermore, these items can be used as reference points in any cover letter and resumé that you submit.

In addition to the general purposes listed above, professional portfolios can serve to support other professional goals. Consider the following specific uses for a professional portfolio as defined by Simmons and Lumsden (n.d.).

MARKETING YOUR SKILLS IN JOB INTERVIEWS

The professional portfolio can be used as part of the interview process to showcase your abilities and accomplishments to a potential employer. The job history and descriptions and other information included on a resumé represent important information that a potential employer definitely needs. The examples of completed work (referred to as *artifacts*) included in the portfolio demonstrate your technical ability, attention to detail, organizational skills, information management abilities, and communication skills.

Your portfolio serves as a vehicle for demonstrating your skills and showcasing your accomplishments to potential employers.

DOCUMENTING PROFESSIONAL DEVELOPMENT ACTIVITIES

If you are in a field that requires licensure or certification, it is likely that you must submit evidence of continued professional development to keep your credentials current. Institutional and programmatic accrediting bodies typically require evidence of continuing professional development. In addition, there may be other circumstances in which you will be asked for evidence of your lifelong learning efforts. The professional portfolio can provide the documentation of these activities for a variety of regulatory agencies.

GUIDING YOUR PROFESSIONAL DEVELOPMENT

In addition to documenting your continued learning for the purposes of career advancement and regulatory compliance, the professional portfolio provides you with a guide for your personal growth and development. Chapter 1 discussed the process of finding your niche in your field. Creating an effective portfolio can result in your having a tool for recognizing trends in your professional development, setting goals, and developing your professional interests and skills.

SUPPORTING REQUESTS FOR SALARY INCREASES OR PROMOTIONS

The step after becoming established in a position is often to seek a salary increase or to apply for a promotion. In either case, it is important to be able to document your accomplishments to substantiate your request for an increased salary or to demonstrate your ability to assume the additional responsibilities of a promotion. Carefully selected items in the portfolio can demonstrate merit for a raise as well as qualifications for a promotion.

QUALIFYING FOR BONUSES AND OTHER FINANCIAL AWARDS

As with raises and promotions, a portfolio of your achievements can document professional development activities that may be required to be considered for bonuses. Receiving grants for program development and research may also require documentation of your professional activities.

 ## TYPES OF PORTFOLIOS

Several types of portfolios can be used to serve a range of purposes. Although the various types are usually maintained as separate pieces, elements of each can be used to culminate in a professional portfolio. Three types of portfolios that can be utilized throughout your academic experience and transformed into a professional portfolio for interviewing will be reviewed here.

THE LEARNING OR DEVELOPMENTAL PORTFOLIO

Barrett (2001) and Springfield (n.d.) discuss the learning and developmental portfolios, respectively. Artifacts in these types of portfolios serve the purpose of documenting your development over time. They typically include written reflections on what you have learned and how your learning contributes to your professional development, and they are kept on an ongoing basis to document development. Springfield

> ## success steps for creating an effective learning or developmental portfolio
>
> - Select artifacts that illustrate your development over time.
> - Include reflections on what you have learned and how artifacts contribute to your professional growth.
> - Refine materials into a finished format when you want to include them in a professional portfolio.

(n.d.) points out that the personal and "unrefined" nature of the material in this type of portfolio usually renders it inappropriate for use in an interview or other professional situation. It may be possible, however, to translate some of the material from the developmental portfolio into a piece that supports the professional portfolio. Developmental portfolios can be continued throughout your career as a vehicle for reflection and personal growth. Developmental or learning portfolios may also be called "working," "reflective," or "self-assessment" portfolios.

THE ASSESSMENT PORTFOLIO

Assessment portfolios are collections of work that demonstrate achievement in a course, program, or project (Barrett, 2001; Springfield, n.d.). Assessment portfolios can be effective measures of "soft" skills such as critical thinking and problem solving; reflective and self-assessment processes may also be a large component of the assessment portfolio. Like the developmental portfolio, some of the material may be too unrefined for inclusion in a professional portfolio; however, the content of these less refined items may contribute to the more polished artifacts to be presented in professional circumstances.

> ## success steps for creating an effective assessment portfolio
>
> - Focus on one area of professional development.
> - Include artifacts that illustrate your development in this area.
> - Include reflections on how the activities have contributed to your growth in the area of focus.
> - Refine materials into a finished format to be included in a professional portfolio.

success steps for creating an effective professional portfolio

- Include examples of your best work and highest achievements.
- Use portfolio materials to support your resumé and the presentation you make to a potential employer.
- Relate reflections to a specific professional goal or achievement.

THE PROFESSIONAL OR CAREER PORTFOLIO

The professional or career portfolio is the main focus of this chapter. This type of portfolio represents your best work and examples of your highest achievements. These are the polished pieces that will effectively market you to a potential employer or represent your accomplishments in other professional circumstances. Springfield (n.d.) suggests that you use items from the developmental and assessment portfolios as contributing material to your professional presentation. Also, if you use reflection or assessment items, use each one for a specific purpose and relate each to a specific goal or accomplishment.

TABLE 5-1 TYPES OF PORTFOLIOS

Type of Portfolio	Uses	Important Elements
The Learning or Developmental Portfolio	Documents learning and professional development over time	Artifacts: ▶ document a sequence of learning or professional progress in a specific area. ▶ typically include written reflections on what you have learned and how your learning contributes to your professional development.
The Assessment Portfolio	Demonstrates achievement in a course, program, or project	Artifacts: ▶ can assess "soft" skills such as critical thinking and problem solving. ▶ typically include reflective and self-assessment processes.
The Professional or Career Portfolio	Represents best work and examples of highest achievements	Artifacts: ▶ are the polished pieces that will effectively market skills to a potential employer. ▶ represent accomplishments relevant to professional circumstances.

Use all three types of portfolios, shown in Table 5-1, to contribute to your professional development, both in school and in your career. Remember that all types of portfolios can be effectively used in all stages of your career. For example, a developmental portfolio can document your ongoing professional growth and learning after graduation. An assessment portfolio can document your achievement in a continuing education course. As you develop professionally, your career or professional portfolio of accomplishments will also change. Use the various types of portfolios during different stages of your career to best achieve your current professional goal.

SELF-ASSESSMENT QUESTIONS

- How could you use a portfolio to enhance your learning immediately?
- How might you use a portfolio in the future?

apply it

Portfolio Research

GOAL: To increase your familiarity with different portfolios and their uses

STEP 1: Conduct an Internet search using the terms "professional portfolios" or "career portfolios." Review the results for articles that will be helpful to you.

STEP 2: Create a file of important tips and ideas that you find in the articles. Consider creating a file of hard copies of the articles or bookmark them in an electronic file. Use your file as a reference when creating your own portfolio.

STEP 3: Consider sharing and exchanging resources with classmates who are also completing this activity.

STEP 4: Add your list of resources to your learning portfolio.

apply it

Beginnings of a Professional Portfolio

GOAL: To start a professional portfolio that can be used in the job search process

STEP 1: Using the steps outlined in this chapter, devise a plan for creating your professional portfolio. You may also use the results from the other activities in this chapter for this process.

STEP 2: Research and find the resources you will need to create the artifacts that you wish to include. For example, if you want to include a DVD in your portfolio, how will you create it?

STEP 3: Begin assembling the materials and resources that you will need to complete your professional portfolio. Realize that this is a long-term endeavor. It is helpful to view this activity as a process over time.

STEP 4: Consider keeping the developing artifacts, or a record of developing the artifacts, in your Learning Portfolio.

5

5

PORTFOLIO FORMATS

Professional portfolios can be in electronic format, hard copy, or presented in a combination of both formats. Each has its advantages and disadvantages, and the format you select will depend on your field, the type of material you are presenting, and your intended audience. Various formats are presented in the following paragraphs; select the most appropriate based on your situation.

ELECTRONIC FORMATS

Electronic portfolios are those that use a variety of electronic technologies such as videotapes, sound bites, and other visual or audio enhancements, including computer-readable media (Barrett, 2001). Barrett differentiates the electronic portfolio from the digital portfolio, in which all elements are in computer-readable form only, and lists the following advantages of the electronic portfolio:

▶ More easily stored and uses minimal storage space

▶ Easily updated and backed up

▶ Efficiently transported or transmitted electronically

▶ Increases and demonstrates your technical skills

▶ May be more appropriate in highly technical fields

Disadvantages include the following:

▶ The recipient must have the equipment to use the electronic item.

▶ The recipient must have compatible software for digital media.

▶ The recipient must have the expertise to use electronic formats.

▶ Electronic portfolios may not be appreciated or effectively reviewed in less technical fields.

A wide variety of online portfolio tools are available to help guide you in the design of your professional portfolio. Before you begin to develop yours, consider consulting with Career Services at your school to see whether they can provide you with examples. Alternatively, an Internet search should yield examples as well. Customize your search to your area of study.

Stewart Cohen/Getty Images

Your choice of a method for presenting your portfolio will depend on the type of material, your audience, and other considerations specific to your field.

HARD COPY PORTFOLIOS

Hard copy portfolios are collections of documents and other media. Many hard copy portfolios are organized in a three-ring binder, which is recommended so that the contents can be easily changed and revised (Shalaway, 1999). Some of the advantages of the hard copy portfolio are listed here:

- Easy reading, due to traditional format
- Requires no special equipment or expertise
- May be more appropriate in fields where technology is not a typical medium of communication

Disadvantages include these:

- Bulkiness; more difficult to transport or send
- Takes up a greater amount of storage space
- May be seen as outdated in highly technical fields

photocay/Alamy

Portfolios can be presented in an electronic format, hard copy, or a combination of both.

COMBINATION PORTFOLIOS

You may have some portfolio artifacts that lend themselves to an electronic format and others that are more appropriate in hard copy. Consider the advantages and disadvantages of each, as well as the format that will present the information most effectively. If possible, find out as much as you can about the individual who is reviewing the portfolio and his or her preferences. Finally, consider other elements that are unique and relevant to your situation. Weigh all of these factors in determining the most effective format for your portfolio.

5

CASE IN POINT: SHOW AND TELL

Read the scenario below. Then, in groups or as a class, discuss the questions at the end.

Lily Blackstone has numerous projects and documents that she has accumulated over the course of her academic studies. These items represent her achievements and abilities in a competitive job market. Lily would like to include these

continued

5

continued

examples of her accomplishments in her interviewing process. She is wondering how to do this in a manner that is appropriate and professional.

▶ How can Lily appropriately showcase her projects and achievements as part of the interviewing process?

▶ What criteria should Lily follow when selecting projects and documents to showcase? How should she determine the criteria?

▶ How should Lily present her portfolio to potential employers?

CONTENTS OF THE PORTFOLIO

Professional portfolios typically contain items commonly used to document professional development. Simmons and Lumsden (n.d.) suggest putting the following artifacts in a professional portfolio:

▶ Resumé or curriculum vitae

▶ Transcripts

▶ Documentation of professional memberships and affiliations

▶ Documentation of professional licensure and other credentials

▶ Letter of reference and recommendations

▶ Documentation of specific skills, such as speeches, acceptance letters for presentations, awards, and other commendations

▶ Samples of work, such as reports, designs, completed projects or their outcomes, and other tangible results of your efforts. Note that certain work samples may be best presented in person; others, electronically. This is an example of when you will need to select the best format for your material.

Contents should be presented neatly, correctly, and professionally. Carefully review portfolio contents for appearance and accuracy. Portfolios should be reviewed with the same level of critical objectivity that one would use in reviewing a resumé or other professional document.

? CRITICAL THINKING QUESTION

▶ Considering your field and situation, which format would best fit your needs? (Consider electronic, hard copy, or a combination.) Explain the rationale for your choice.

SELECTING ARTIFACTS

Selecting the contents of the portfolio should be a thoughtful process focused on achieving your objective. The completed portfolio should clearly illustrate the story you are telling about yourself. It should be organized in a logical order rather than being a haphazard group of documents collected in one place (Shalaway, 1999). The artifacts that you select for your portfolio will depend on the portfolio type, its intended use, and your objectives. In general, ask yourself the following questions when determining which artifacts to include in your portfolio:

▶ What is my objective in creating this portfolio? What am I documenting?

▶ Which of my work samples will reflect what I desire to document?

THE PROFESSIONAL OR CAREER PORTFOLIO

When compiling a professional or career portfolio, select artifacts that demonstrate your professional abilities. Ask yourself the following questions of each artifact:

▶ Is the artifact of excellent quality?

▶ Is the artifact polished and professional?

▶ Does the artifact reflect and document the development of skills required for the position?

▶ How do reflections and assessment materials contribute to my objective?

▶ Are reflections and assessments presented appropriately and professionally?

THE LEARNING OR DEVELOPMENTAL PORTFOLIO

When compiling a learning or developmental portfolio, artifacts should reflect your progress toward a specific goal. The following questions can help you determine artifacts to include in your developmental portfolio:

▶ Does the artifact demonstrate a significant step in professional growth?

▶ Is the artifact relevant to the skills needed for a specific goal?

Review, and ask others to review, your portfolio contents carefully to ensure accuracy, thoroughness, and a professional presentation.

© Monkey Business Images /Shutterstock.com

5

- Do the reflections that you include relate to the professional developmental process?
- Do the reflections demonstrate thoughtfulness and insight about your own growth and goal achievement?

THE ASSESSMENT PORTFOLIO

Assessment portfolios are intended to demonstrate achievement of specific objectives, such as completion of a project or course. Because artifacts included in this type of portfolio are intended to show progress and assess your growth, the artifacts may not be "perfect" initially. Artifacts may include assessments of your progress over time, and your reflections will show evidence of your learning and development. Answering the following questions can help you determine content for an assessment portfolio:

- Is the artifact related to achievement of the objective?
- Does the artifact show progress toward the objective?
- Do assessments demonstrate progress toward the objective?
- Do reflections demonstrate an awareness of professional growth toward the objective?
- Does the artifact reflect and document the development of skills related to the objective?

Use the following table to determine the contents for the type of portfolio you have chosen.

apply it

Entry-Level Position Requirements

GOAL: To determine appropriate examples of work to include in a professional portfolio

STEP 1: Research an entry-level position in your field. Consider a specialty area that interests you. Focus on the skills that employers require and prefer for someone entering that particular specialty.

STEP 2: Review your courses, assignments, and projects. Select those assignments that best reflect the skills that are required.

STEP 3: Decide how you would best represent these projects in a professional portfolio. For example, would you select an electronic or hard copy format? What elements of the finished project would you include to demonstrate your skills?

STEP 4: Consider keeping your developing professional portfolio artifacts in your Learning Portfolio.

CHECKLIST FOR PORTFOLIO CONTENTS

Type of Portfolio	Contents Checklist
General Portfolio Considerations	▶ What is my objective in creating this portfolio? What am I documenting?
	▶ Which of my work examples will reflect that which I desire to document?
The Professional or Career Portfolio	▶ Is the artifact of excellent quality?
	▶ Is the artifact polished and professional?
	▶ Does the artifact reflect and document the development of skills required for the position?
	▶ If I include reflections or assessment material, how do they contribute to my objective?
	▶ Are reflections and assessments presented appropriately and professionally?
The Learning or Developmental Portfolio	▶ Does the artifact demonstrate a significant step in professional growth?
	▶ Is the artifact related to the skills related to a specific goal?
	▶ Do any reflections that you include relate to the professional developmental process?
	▶ Do reflections demonstrate thoughtfulness and insight about your own growth and goal achievement?
The Assessment Portfolio	▶ Is the artifact related to achievement of the objective?
	▶ Does the artifact show progress toward the objective?
	▶ Do assessments demonstrate progress toward the objective?
	▶ Do reflections demonstrate an awareness of professional growth toward the objective?
	▶ Do the artifacts reflect and document the development of skills related to the objective?

apply it

Preparing for the Professional Portfolio

GOAL: To gather potential artifacts for the professional portfolio

STEP 1: Using the information in this chapter, prepare a list of potential items specific to your field that you would include in your professional portfolio.

STEP 2: Research credentials and other requirements of your field. Professional organizations and state licensing boards are usually good sources for this information.

STEP 3: Construct a chart or timeline that indicates the criteria for achieving the credential and the time frame for achieving it. Pay special attention to those credentials that are required for entrance into professional practice or those that would enhance your chances of obtaining your position of choice.

STEP 4: Create a checklist of steps you need to take to complete each credential. Include contact information and deadlines related to each step.

STEP 5: Consider including the checklist in your Learning Portfolio and referring to it as a guide for compiling this aspect of your professional portfolio.

ORGANIZING THE PORTFOLIO

Portfolios should be organized in a manner that supports the "story" you are telling. Simmons and Lumsden (n.d.) suggest that most portfolios are organized functionally or chronologically. Your choice of organization will depend on the type of portfolio and its objective.

FUNCTIONAL ORGANIZATION

Functionally organized portfolios are arranged by skill area. For example, if you wish to showcase your management skills, then artifacts demonstrating these skills would be grouped together. Functional organization of a portfolio is similar to the functional resumé, which lists achievements according to skill area. Functional organization is appropriate for professional portfolios or for a developmental portfolio that documents your development in a set of areas. Assessment portfolios may be organized by topic to document achievement by function.

CHRONOLOGICAL ORGANIZATION

Portfolios that are organized chronologically are arranged according to the sequence in which the artifacts were completed or milestones were achieved. For example, a portfolio showing progress in a single course might be organized with artifacts from the beginning of the course through the end. Chronological portfolios can be used as one would use a chronological resumé (achievements listed in the order they were accomplished) and are commonly used to demonstrate development and growth over time.

EVALUATING THE PORTFOLIO

It is important to evaluate the effectiveness of your portfolio in terms of how it meets its intended objective. Portfolio evaluation should occur before you present it in professional circumstances, in order to ensure that it is complete and appropriately configured. Evaluation methods should also be used periodically to ensure that your portfolio is keeping pace with your professional growth. Evaluate your portfolio by answering the following questions:

▸ How completely were my objectives met? What evidence do I have to show that my objectives were met? *How* were they met?

apply it

Portfolio Evaluation Checklist

GOAL: To prepare a targeted evaluation checklist for professional portfolios

STEP 1: Form a small group of students from your class.

STEP 2: Using the general portfolio evaluation checklist on page 118, expand the evaluation to be more detailed and specific to your field. Create your evaluation items based on criteria appropriate to someone entering your field. Consider what an employer would desire and create items that will guide and evaluate the selection of artifacts accordingly.

STEP 3: Consider including the finished evaluation form in your Learning Portfolio.

▶ Does the organization of the portfolio serve its purpose?

▶ Do the artifacts effectively tell my story? Do I need to add any artifacts? Should any be removed?

▶ What responses and comments does an objective reviewer provide about the portfolio's contents?

CHECKLIST FOR PORTFOLIO EVALUATION

▶ How completely were my objectives met?

▶ What evidence do I have to show how they were met?

▶ Does the organization of the portfolio serve its purpose?

▶ Do the artifacts effectively tell the "story" that is intended?

▶ Should any artifacts be added?

▶ Should any artifacts be removed?

SELF-ASSESSMENT QUESTION

• What other criteria might you use to evaluate the effectiveness of your portfolio?

CHAPTER SUMMARY

This chapter introduced you to professional portfolios as a tool for showcasing your professional skills and achievements. You learned various types of portfolios, appropriate contents for each, and how to use each type of portfolio effectively. The goal and purpose of the portfolio was a major theme throughout the chapter, and you received guidelines for selecting artifacts based on the purpose of the portfolio. Portfolio formats and organization were also emphasized, and you received guidelines for selecting an appropriate format and effectively arranging portfolio contents.

POINTS TO KEEP IN MIND

In this chapter, numerous main points were discussed in detail:

▶ The general purpose of the portfolio is to provide examples of the work an individual is capable of.

▶ Portfolios can serve different purposes. The types of portfolios include the professional or career portfolio, the developmental or learning portfolio, and the assessment portfolio.

▶ Professional portfolios can serve to support other professional goals, such as obtaining salary increases and promotions, achieving professional credentials, and qualifying for professional development milestones and awards.

▶ Professional portfolios can be in electronic format, hard copy, or a combination of both.

▶ Professional portfolios typically contain items commonly used to document professional development, such as a resumé, transcripts, documentation of recognition, and examples of work.

▶ Selecting the contents of the portfolio should be a thoughtful process directed toward achieving your objective. The completed portfolio should clearly illustrate the story you are telling about yourself.

▶ Portfolios are typically organized functionally or chronologically. Portfolios should be organized in a manner that supports the story you are telling.

▶ It is important to evaluate the effectiveness of your portfolio in terms of how it meets its intended objective. Evaluation can occur prior to using the portfolio to ensure its completeness and after its use to determine its effectiveness.

CHECK YOUR UNDERSTANDING

Visit www.cengagebrain.com to see how well you have mastered the material in Chapter 5.

SUGGESTED ITEMS FOR LEARNING PORTFOLIO

▶ Portfolio Research: This activity will help you to select the right portfolio for your needs by increasing your familiarity with different portfolios and their uses.

▶ Preparing for the Professional Portfolio: The goal of this activity is to gather potential artifacts for the professional portfolio.

▶ Entry-Level Position Requirements: This activity will help you determine appropriate examples of work to include in a professional portfolio.

▶ Portfolio Evaluation Checklists: These activities will help you to prepare a targeted evaluation checklist for professional portfolios.

▶ Beginnings of a Professional Portfolio: The goal of this activity is to help you start a professional portfolio that can be used in the job search process.

REFERENCES

Barrett, H. C. (2001). Electronic portfolios [Electronic version]. *Educational Technology: An Encyclopedia.* ABC-CLIO. Retrieved May 6, 2013, from http://electronicportfolios.com/portfolios/encyclopediaentry.htm

Internweb.com. (n.d.). Portfolios: A secret weapon for your internship search. Retrieved May 6, 2013, from http://www.internweb.com/portfolios.asp

Shalaway, L. (1999). The professional portfolio. Excerpted from L. Beech (Ed.), *Learning to teach…not just for beginners.* New York: Scholastic, Inc. Retrieved May 6, 2013, from http://www2.scholastic.com/browse/article.jsp?id=4148

Simmons, A., & Lumsden, J. (n.d.). Portfolio preparation guide. Florida State University, Career Center. Retrieved May 6, 2013, from http://www.career.fsu.edu/experience/document/portfolio-guide.html

Springfield, E. (n.d.). Student portfolio uses. University of Michigan School of Nursing. Retrieved May 6, 2013, from http://www-personal.umich.edu/~espring/ePort/stuPfolios.html

5

CHAPTER OUTLINE

Compassionate Eye Foundation/David Leahy/Digital Vision/Getty Images

6

Professionalism in the Job Search

LEARNING OBJECTIVES

By the end of this chapter, you will achieve the following objectives:

▶ Define professionalism as it pertains to the job search process.

▶ Describe the process of professional socialization and employ steps in the professional socialization process.

▶ Explain the importance of utilizing proper etiquette during the job search.

▶ Discuss ways that job applicants can demonstrate good manners.

▶ Describe the considerations that a job applicant should make when using a cell phone for an interview.

▶ Discuss the standards of effective phone interviewing.

▶ Explain important considerations to make when an interview is conducted over a meal.

▶ Demonstrate the ability to use good phone manners during a phone interview.

▶ Explain important considerations to make when an interview is conducted via video chat.

▶ Describe appropriate clothing to be worn to an interview.

▶ Understand how first impressions can affect the opinions of others.

▶ Explain how outward appearance can affect internal confidence.

▶ Discuss considerations that should be given to interviewing attire.

▶ Discuss grooming tips that are important to adhere to as a professional.

BE IN THE KNOW

Don't Tweet an Interview or Job Away

Want to show professionalism in both your job search and on the job? A recent survey on professionalism asked human resources managers about Information Technology use in the workplace and found that abuses on the job are rampant. The predominant four problems reported are:

- Excessive tweeting/use of Facebook 82.5%
- Text messaging at inappropriate times 81.9%
- Inappropriate use of the Internet 78.1%
- Excessive use of cell phones for personal calls 65.0% (The Center for Professional Excellence at York College of Pennsylvania, 2012).

Make a conscious effort to curb your enthusiasm for cell phone use, social media, texting, and Internet abuse while conducting your job search or while on the job. These kinds of habits can—and will—hurt you in the long run.

WHAT IS PROFESSIONALISM?

As you start your career in your field of study, it goes without saying that you must act professionally on the job. This also holds true for the job search process. How you conduct yourself and the image that you portray during the initial contact with a potential employer speaks volumes as to the type of employee you will be once you are hired.

If you have a virtual presence on a business social networking site such as LinkedIn, make sure that it is professional and formal in appearance. It should be free of grammatical, punctuation, and capitalization errors, says James Yoakum of MentorWorks. "Nothing can derail a job search effort faster than the lack of professionalism" (Yoakum, 2009). It is also important to make sure that you monitor more informal social networking sites for what you post and disclose about yourself. Additionally, your business e-mail address should be straightforward and contain both your first and last name within the body of the address. Your home or cell phone greeting should also be straightforward and not contain any frivolous or opinioned remarks.

Your social networking, e-mail, and voice mail contact information says much about you. Make sure as you embark on your job search and career that the message you send to a prospective employer is professional.

PROFESSIONAL SOCIALIZATION

? CRITICAL THINKING QUESTIONS

Professional socialization is "a process by which individuals learn the knowledge, skills, values, roles, and attitudes associated with their professional responsibilities" (Pitney, 2002, Introduction, para. 1). Teschendorf and Nemshick (2001) discuss how professional socialization is a gradual process that involves effort. Although professional socialization has traditionally been emphasized in the healthcare professions, the concepts of professional socialization apply to all employees who are developing their professional identity and establishing their place within their field.

Your professional socialization process will be unique and will involve your becoming acquainted with both formal and informal aspects of your field and the organization for which you work. Consider the following guidelines to facilitate your professional socialization process, adapted from the works of Teschendorf and Nemshick (2001), Pitney (2002), and Deal and Kennedy (2000):

▶ **Establish reliable information sources.** Reliable information about your profession or organization can come from your professional organization, a trusted individual, or a combination of dependable sources. From these sources, pay attention to the expected behaviors and attitudes of your field and/or organization and how these are demonstrated in daily activities.

▶ **Pay attention to role models.** Another technique for becoming socialized into your professional role is to observe individuals who are experienced and successful in the profession or organization. There is much to be gained by informal learning, such as observing accepted practices and incorporating them (with judgment) into your own behaviors. Ensure that role models meet the criterion of being a reliable source.

▶ **Understand the history and current status of your profession and organization.** Learning the history and current status of your profession or organization provides insight into its rituals, values, authority distribution, work relationships, politics, and communication practices. Understanding these processes and finding your role within them will support your transition into a new environment.

- ▶ How can a set of professional values be instilled in a large group such as an organization or profession?
- ▶ How can you ensure that your decisions and actions are ethical?
- ▶ What happens when your personal values come into conflict with those of your profession or the values of the organization that hired you?
- ▶ How will you resolve conflicts between your personal and professional values?

6

▶ **Know professional standards.** Your profession is likely to have standards for how tasks are to be accomplished and ideas that have been established and accepted. Professional socialization includes adopting these standards into daily practice. Standards are based on professional values and ethics, so it is important to understand the values underlying your profession as well as its code of ethics. Some professions incorporate practice and ethical expectations into one comprehensive document. An example is *Ethics and Ethics Standards* (The American Occupational Therapy Association [AOTA], 2010) of the occupational therapy profession. Other professions may have similar documents or standards that are less formally stated.

▶ **Look for professional socialization opportunities.** There are numerous opportunities that provide both formal and informal learning. Some examples that are frequently available to students include information from your academic training, organizational orientations, and other organized learning situations, such as participating in a work environment as part of academic preparation. Chapter 2 emphasized the internship, which has been identified as an effective method of professional socialization.

▶ **Join professional organizations.** Consider becoming a member of your field's professional organization or the student division of the professional organization. For example, public relations students can join the Public Relations Society of America (PRSA) or the Public Relations Student Society of America (PRSSA). Professional organizations frequently offer material and information specifically for students, can be a source of scholarships, and offer an opportunity to become involved with activities in your field. Many organizations offer reduced membership rates for students.

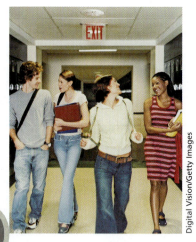

Digital Vision/Getty Images

6

Casual and comfortable dress may be fine for campus life, but to make a positive first impression on potential employers, professional attire is a must. Casual campus dress such as that in the picture is not appropriate for an interview.

success steps for facilitating the professional socialization process

- Establish reliable information sources.
- Pay attention to role models.
- Understand the history and current status of your profession and organization.
- Know professional standards.
- Look for professional socialization opportunities.

THE IMPORTANCE OF ETIQUETTE IN THE JOB SEARCH

Something as simple as etiquette—good manners—can seem like an insignificant thing. However, the social appropriateness that you demonstrate in the job search speaks to your professionalism and how you will manage your conduct on the job. An employer appreciates being treated courteously, and doing so makes a favorable impression. In addition, consider the messages that etiquette sends.

▶ **How you will represent the organization.** The consideration and courtesy that you demonstrate during the job search process provides the employer with an example of how you will treat customers or clients. The way in which clients are treated forms the public image of the company and either attracts business or discourages it. Employers want to hire individuals who will represent their company in a positive manner.

▶ **Messages about you as a person.** The consideration that you show others contributes to the reputation you are building as a professional. Professional circles are frequently small, and word travels. Even if a particular employer does not hire you, your reputation is being established based on your interactions and your manners.

6

apply it

The Importance of Proper Etiquette

GOAL: *To gain an understanding of the importance that employers place on applicants utilizing proper etiquette*

STEP 1: Schedule an interview with a professional in your chosen field. The purpose of the interview is to inquire as to the importance that the employer places on proper etiquette and how proper etiquette should be exhibited by job applicants.

STEP 2: Write a short report regarding your findings and be prepared to share it with the class.

STEP 3: Consider placing the report regarding the Importance of Proper Etiquette in your Learning Portfolio.

JOB SEARCH ETIQUETTE

Professionalism can be demonstrated in various ways, including the use of proper etiquette. There are many opportunities for job applicants to demonstrate proper etiquette throughout the application process. It is important to remember that employers not only seek a technically qualified individual, but also look for an individual who has the capability to follow general principles of good manners and professionalism. The following are some general guidelines that a job applicant can utilize to demonstrate good manners (Search Job Careers, n.d.).

▶ **Respond immediately to any communication received from an employer.** Follow up the employer's call, letter, or e-mail and inform the employer whether you are accepting or declining the invitation. Do not be rude by neglecting to follow through. Even if you are not interested in working for the company, you need to inform the employer of this decision. It is important to do so graciously and maintain a positive professional relationship throughout the process of withdrawing an application or declining an offer.

▶ **Never be late.** If an employer tells you to call at a certain time, then make sure you call on time. Show up for the interview on time or even a little early. Being on time demonstrates respect for the other person's time.

▶ **Demonstrate politeness.** Politeness can be demonstrated by saying words such as *please, thank you,* and *excuse me.* Say "thank you" and "please" to the receptionist and other individuals with whom you have contact. Remember the importance of establishing good first impressions.

▶ **Pay attention to time.** Be aware of rambling. Employers are busy individuals who want applicants to answer questions clearly and concisely. During your conversations and interviews with the employer, be mindful of his or her time. Glancing discreetly at one's watch is appropriate. Quickly come to a stopping point if you see time is running out. The employer will greatly appreciate your attention to this matter. If the employer chooses to extend the time, that is his or her choice. The job applicant should be willing to stay as long as the employer requires.

6

▌ **Listen well.** Employers want to share information about the company and the job with applicants. Although some of the information may be public knowledge, show your interest. Never yawn or stare off into space, as doing so demonstrates poor manners.

▌ **Be aware of your body language.** Sit up and demonstrate attentiveness. Straight yet relaxed posture with a slightly forward lean, direct eye contact, and an occasional nod communicate enthusiasm and interest. In addition to interest, direct eye contact indicates honesty. Avoid crossing your arms, as doing so can be interpreted as anger or a closed attitude. Positive body language communicates much about your attitude and how you are approaching the employment opportunity.

▌ **Demonstrate passion and interest in the company and the job.** Actions such as making follow-up calls to learn the status of the interviewing and decision-making processes demonstrate your investment. Take the initiative to bring to the interview items such as a portfolio of your work to demonstrate your abilities and dedication to your work. The more you demonstrate passion for the company and the job, the more the employer will see you as a potential candidate.

▌ **For any interview, be prepared.** A lack of preparedness can indicate a lack of interest. If an employer asks whether you have any questions, make sure you do! Those who fail to ask questions can be viewed as uninterested.

▌ **Perform a job-related task if asked.** Some employers will have applicants perform a job-related task to see whether the applicant is qualified for the job. Graciously perform the task to the best of your ability and never refuse to perform the task requested by the employer. Refusal indicates lack of confidence and lack of ability.

▌ **Send a postinterview thank-you note.** A survey conducted by the staffing firm Accountemps found that "more than 76% of employers like receiving a postinterview thank-you note, but only 36% of applicants write them" (Search Job Careers, n.d.). Thank-you notes should be sent immediately after the interview. The content of the thank-you note should include thanking the interviewer for his or her time, offering to provide additional material as needed, and stating an interest in working for the company.

SELF-ASSESSMENT QUESTIONS

- Do you typically demonstrate good manners?
- With what areas of etiquette could you become more familiar?

? CRITICAL THINKING QUESTION

▌ How do you respond to the following statement? "As an employer I would never hire an individual who demonstrates poor manners."

▌ **Never renege on an agreement you make with a company.**
When you have accepted a position with an organization, you must stop interviewing with other companies. The employer is depending on you and has possibly lost the chance to hire their second choice due to the time that has passed. In addition, word travels in the professional world and you may be hurting your reputation.

success steps for proper etiquette in the job search

- Respond immediately to any communication received from an employer.
- Be on time for any interview or appointment with an employer.
- Demonstrate politeness by demonstrating courtesies such as saying "please," "thank you," and "excuse me," and waiting to be offered a seat.
- Pay attention to time and be aware of rambling. Speak succinctly and to the point.
- Listen well. Pay attention to information about the organization and show interest in what the employer tells you.
- Be aware of your body language.
- Demonstrate passion and interest in the company and the job.
- For any interview, be prepared. Use the research you have completed on the company and have questions ready to demonstrate your interest.
- Some employers will have applicants perform a job-related task to see whether the applicant is qualified for the job. Graciously perform the task.
- Send a postinterview thank-you note.
- Never renege on an agreement you make with a company.

6

CASE IN POINT: CALL ME MAYBE

Read the scenario below. Then, in groups or as a class, discuss the questions at the end.

Nearing the end of her college education, Joan has sent out letters of application to a number of employers. Today, Joan received a call from an employer who had received her information and wants to conduct an initial interview by phone. The interview is scheduled for tomorrow at 2:00 P.M.

▶ How should Joan prepare for the phone interview?

▶ Should Joan prepare differently for the phone interview as opposed to an in-person interview? If so, how?

▶ What considerations should Joan make to ensure that the interview runs smoothly?

▶ What phone courtesies should Joan demonstrate?

▶ If Joan is using a cell phone, what are the additional considerations? What should she do differently?

ETIQUETTE IN SPECIAL INTERVIEW SITUATIONS

General etiquette considerations are important in all professional interactions and activities. There are situations that may arise during the job search process that require attention to specific details that are unique to the situation. Traditional interviewing will be covered in Chapter 7. The following less traditional interviewing methods are included here because of their unique demands and the special etiquette considerations they require.

PHONE INTERVIEW ETIQUETTE

Demonstrating phone etiquette is an important element of the job search process. Initial contact with a company often occurs by phone. Increasingly, the human resources department calls the contact numbers job applicants provide on their resumés in a prescreening process. The importance of this information being accurate is critical to job search success. Voice mailboxes are frequently used to receive messages. Job applicants must ensure that these devices are set up with an appropriate message that demonstrates both professionalism and proper manners. Entertaining messages that may be amusing to your friends are not always appropriate when you are expecting return calls from prospective employers. Change any whimsical messages to something straightforward and professional. Proper messages include examples such as those listed here (Crawford Hentz, n.d.[a], "Pre-contact"):

▶ "You've reached Brenda, Cathy, and Mark. Please leave a message."

▶ "You've reached the Sizemores. Please leave a message."

▶ "You've reached 617-973-XXXX. Please leave a message."

If you rely on other people to take messages for you, it is your responsibility to ensure that these individuals also understand and use proper phone etiquette and take messages accurately.

When you receive a message from an employer, phone etiquette requires you to return the message in a timely manner. When returning the call, it is important to give your full first and last name, along with the reason for your call. Always be polite and repeat information as required. Be aware of rate of your voice and pitch. Speak clearly and distinctly.

If you receive a call from an employer directly, don't defer the employer. It is best to put aside what you are doing and take the call promptly. However, there may be circumstances when you are preoccupied with another task or rushing to get to an appointment and are truly unable to give your undivided attention. In this case, it may be best not to take the call and return the call when you are able to focus. If you answer the phone, good phrases to use in this situation would be "I'm so happy you called. I have about 10 minutes before I have to run out the door. Is that enough time, or can I call you back later this afternoon?" This way, you are expressing your interest, being clear about the time you have, and suggesting a time to connect later (Crawford Hentz, n.d.[a], "When you're there for the contact").

CELL PHONE INTERVIEW ETIQUETTE

With the increased use of cell phones versus land lines, job applicants do need to make sure that cell phones are fully charged when possible. If the battery is low, inform the employer at the beginning of the call and ask whether you can call him or her back immediately using a different phone. If you use a cell phone as your primary phone, inform the employer at the time of the call and indicate that a call back will be immediate if a disconnect occurs. Make sure to get correct call-back numbers. If hearing the employer is difficult due to a poor cell phone signal, check that you understand each other. Crawford Hentz (n.d.[a]), "When you're there for the contact") suggests saying, "I'm having trouble hearing you. Can you hear me clearly?" It is less acceptable to ask the employer to speak up, which can sound abrupt and demanding. At the end of the call, make sure to thank the employer for his or her time and follow up the phone call with a thank-you letter.

Phone interviews should be treated with as much care and attention as you would give to an in-person interview. Although getting hired solely from the phone interview is unlikely, it does offer the opportunity for the employer to get to know you and to draw conclusions about whether further conversations should occur.

For further information regarding successful phone interviewing, consider the following recommendations from Crawford Hentz (n.d.[b]):

- ❯ Ensure that the contact information in your cover letter and resumé is correct.

- ❯ Make sure your voice mail message is professional.

- ❯ Keep by the phone a list of companies to which you have sent your resumé. That way, you will not be caught off guard when an employer calls.

- ❯ Be prepared for a telephone interview just as you would for an in-person interview. Do your research just as you would for a traditional interview.

- ❯ Find a location where you will not be disrupted during the phone interview.

- ❯ Take notes of your conversation as you would during an in-person interview. Make sure note taking does not get in the way of good listening skills.

- ❯ Indicate whether you are not able to hear the employer. Do so in a courteous manner.

- ❯ Smile during your interview. It will make a difference in how your voice sounds.

- ❯ Never interrupt the interviewer.

- ❯ Accept silence. If you have sufficiently answered a question, silence is acceptable while the interviewer prepares for the next question. Do not fill the silence with meaningless chatter, but you might ask a question that is related to your last response.

- ❯ Avoid sneezing or coughing. If these are unavoidable, say, "Excuse me." Never yawn, chew gum, eat, or drink during an interview.

6

SELF-ASSESSMENT QUESTION

- Do you think you would do well in a phone interview? What areas might you be able to improve in order to be more effective in a phone interview?

? CRITICAL THINKING QUESTION

- ❯ How would individuals with some hearing loss deal with potential phone interviews? How might technology assist in responding to this issue?

▶ Always say "thank you" at the end of the phone interview, indicate your interest, and ask when to expect further word regarding other possible interviews.

success steps for telephone interview etiquette

- Ensure that the contact information in your cover letter and resumé is correct.
- Have a professional-sounding message on your voice mail.
- Keep a list of companies you have contacted by the phone.
- Prepare by researching the company and writing down questions.
- Find a location where you will not be disturbed during the phone interview.
- Take notes.
- Courteously let the employer know whether you cannot hear what he or she is saying.
- Smile during your interview. Your voice will convey a pleasant demeanor.
- Never interrupt the interviewer.
- Accept silence. If you have sufficiently answered a question, allow the interviewer to prepare for the next question. You may ask a question related to your last response, but do not fill the silence with meaningless chatter.
- Avoid sneezing or coughing. If these are unavoidable, say, "Excuse me."
- At the end of the phone interview say, "Thank you," indicate your interest, and ask when to expect word regarding other possible interviews.

6

apply it

Phone Interview Role-Play

GOAL: *To demonstrate the ability to use good phone manners during a phone interview*

STEP 1: Form pairs with other students in your class.

STEP 2: With scenarios provided by the instructor, role-play a phone interview. One student will be the employer and the other student the job applicant. Treat the role-playing seriously, because this activity can help prepare you for real-life phone interviews. After the role-playing is accomplished, the student playing the employer should constructively critique the job applicant on his or her phone manners and phone interviewing abilities. Where could the job applicant improve? What did he or she do right? If needed, redo the role-playing so you can practice and improve on your phone interviewing abilities. Reverse roles to allow for each student to represent the employer and the job applicant.

STEP 3: Write a brief report on what you learned from this activity and consider putting this information in your Learning Portfolio.

MEALTIME INTERVIEW ETIQUETTE

Some employers may choose to have one of the interviews scheduled over breakfast, lunch, or dinner. If this occurs, consider the following:

▶ Do not choose the most expensive item on the menu. Even though the employer will pay for the meal, be reasonable with your selection.

▶ Choose an item on the menu that will not be messy. Avoid finger foods or items that can be sloppy, such as spaghetti and barbecued ribs.

▶ Avoid using black pepper. Pepper can get stuck in teeth. Use good table manners, such as placing the napkin in your lap prior to beginning the meal, keeping elbows off the table, and using the appropriate utensils.

▶ Never talk with your mouth full. Take small bites and swallow before answering a question.

▶ Use your napkin often to wipe your mouth.

▶ Do not order alcoholic beverages during an interview meal.

▶ After the meal, excuse yourself to go to the restroom. Check for food particles in your teeth before returning to the table.

Further information regarding general table manners can be located on the Internet.

6

success steps for successful mealtime interviewing

- Do not choose the most expensive item on the menu.
- Choose an item on the menu that will not be messy.
- Avoid using pepper, as it can become stuck in your teeth.
- Use good table manners. Place the napkin in your lap prior to beginning the meal, keep elbows off the table, and use the appropriate utensils.
- Take small bites and swallow before answering a question. Never talk with your mouth full.
- Keep your professional appearance by using your napkin to wipe your mouth frequently.
- Do not order alcoholic beverages.
- After the meal, excuse yourself to go to the restroom. Check for food particles in your teeth before returning to the table.

apply it

Mealtime Interviewing

GOAL: To develop a better understanding of how to effectively interview over a meal

STEP 1: Conduct research on the Internet and/or at the library regarding how to effectively interview over a meal.

STEP 2: Write a brief report regarding your findings.

STEP 3: Consider placing the report on Mealtime Interviewing in your Learning Portfolio.

VIDEO CHAT INTERVIEW ETIQUETTE

With the job market becoming increasingly global, and with daily advances in technology, many businesses are turning to video chat to conduct interviews. In addition to the etiquette rules you should follow as with a traditional interview, video chat interview etiquette comes with its own set of unique considerations.

Here are some points to keep in mind before you shake the virtual hand of your interviewer.

- **Dress as you would for a face-to-face interview.** This means professional attire from top to bottom. Do not wear a jacket and tie up top and jeans down below. If you have to stand for some reason during the interview you will give yourself away. This sends an "I do not care" message loud and clear.

- **Check your equipment prior to your session.** Make sure your computer and microphone are in proper working order. Log in to the site at least 10 minutes before your interview start time. Give your interviewer a cell phone number to call in case of a technical issue that cannot be overcome. In this way your interview can still be completed via teleconference.

- **Pay attention to lighting.** Be sure to have good lighting in front of you as opposed to behind you. By doing this your interviewer will be able to see you clearly.

- **Avoid distractions.** Put yourself in a locked room if possible, and let any other household members know about your interview. Turn off any other electronic equipment, such as phones or tablets. Do not have your social networking pages up and running during the interview.

> ### success steps for successful video chat interviewing
>
> - Dress as you would for a face-to-face interview.
> - Check your equipment prior to your session.
> - Pay attention to lighting.
> - Avoid distractions.
> - Review your surroundings.
> - Eye contact and body language are key.
> - Understand the technology.
> - Practice if you can.

▶ **Review your surroundings.** Clean off your desk, close curtains, and get rid of any clutter that might show up on screen. This includes wall posters and the like.

▶ **Eye contact and body language are key.** Make eye contact with your interviewer just as you would in a face-to-face meeting. Keep your hands on the desk or keyboard in front of you. Use correct posture. Keep engaged in the conversation at all times.

▶ **Understand the technology.** With video chat there can be a slight delay between the time you say something and the time there is a response from the other end. Allow for this by not making an additional statement until your previous one was acknowledged.

▶ **Practice if you can.** See if a family member can play the role of the interviewer.

FIRST IMPRESSIONS

When pursuing a job, it is important to recognize the critical nature of making a good first impression. First impressions begin as soon as contact is made with a company of interest. This contact can occur through either written or spoken communication. Impressions are made through your resumé, cover letter, and initial phone call; at the moment you visit to pick up an application; when you walk in for the interview; and when the first and subsequent interviews occur.

> ### success steps for dressing to make a good impression
>
> - Remember that dress and grooming are both critical factors in getting hired.
> - Keep in mind that first impressions *do* matter.
> - Accept that overall dressing and grooming habits have an impact on professional success.

SELF-ASSESSMENT QUESTIONS

- How accurate are your perceptions of the first impressions you give to individuals the first time they meet you?
- What dress and/or grooming habits might you need to improve in order to successfully enter the professional workplace?
- If you have worked as a professional in the past but are now changing careers, what areas can you improve regarding your dress and grooming habits?

? CRITICAL THINKING QUESTION

- What is your reaction to the following statement? "What one wears should not matter as long as the person can do the job."

During all these times, the applicant is being scrutinized and evaluated. Conclusions are being drawn about one's professionalism and personality based on appearance, mannerisms, communication style, attitude, confidence level, and social skills.

Although some individuals may not like the idea that they are being judged by their appearance, it is important to accept certain concepts:

- Dress and grooming are important and are a critical factor in getting hired.
- First impressions do matter.
- Overall dress does affect one's professional success.

Given these facts, it is critical for those who seek success both in obtaining a job and advancing in their careers to work toward improving their fashion sense, style, and grooming habits.

Understanding and accepting that your personal appearance does make a difference is the first step in presenting yourself effectively to potential employers. Developing the skills and presentation necessary to make a good impression is the second step and will be what differentiates a successful individual from one who is less successful. Dress and grooming are significant factors in being hired for a job as well as being considered for advancement within the organization (Wisconsin Department of Workforce Development, 2010).

DRESSING FOR THE INTERVIEW

When deciding on appropriate dress for interviewing, the general consensus is that it is best to dress conservatively. A common standard is to dress one step up from the typical daily attire at the organization.

It may be important to investigate the company where the interview will be taking place to confirm what attire will be appropriate. This can be accomplished by calling and asking someone in the human resources office, checking the company's web site, or by visiting the company prior to the interview. Other considerations that affect dress choice are the type of job being applied for and the company dress expectations. For example, someone who is going to work as an airline mechanic will dress differently for the interview than someone who is applying for an executive position. If the airline mechanic applicant showed up in a three-piece suit, the employer might hesitate in hiring this individual, who is more than likely overdressed for the position. That is not meant to say that the airline mechanic should wear jeans to the interview. In fact, many employers find jeans to be unacceptable interview attire no matter what the job is. Much of the choice regarding what is worn to an interview depends on some common sense and having researched the corporate environment, culture, and the employer's preference.

So, what is acceptable? What if the company employees dress in business casual? Does their dress code affect how you dress for an interview or as a new employee? Does the interviewer's attire determine what you should be wearing? Here are some general thoughts from some professionals:

▶ "The safest look for both men and women in an interview is traditional and conservative" (Brookhaven College Career Development Center, n.d.).

▶ "Appropriate attire supports your image as a person who takes the interview process seriously and understands the nature of the industry in which you are trying to become employed" (Career Services Virginia Tech, 2013).

The most important thing to remember regarding the clothing you select for your interview is that your clothing must not get in the way of your presentation. You are there to sell your skills and abilities. You do not want your clothes to be the focus of the conversation!

GROOMING CONSIDERATIONS

Appropriate interviewing attire does include elements other than a good suit. A neat and clean appearance is perceived by many

> ### success steps for grooming for the interview
>
> - Keep hair neat and clean.
> - Select a hairstyle that complements your face shape and skin tone.
> - Make sure facial hair is groomed or removed.
> - Use deodorant and avoid perfumes and scents.
> - Make sure nails are manicured and appropriately colored if polish is used.
> - Remove body piercings and cover any visible tatoos.

employers as being as important as the choice of dress. The following are grooming suggestions for before the interview:

▶ Hairstyle and care contribute to overall appearance. Hair should be clean and combed into an attractive style. If needed, get a haircut a week or two before the interview. For budget-conscious individuals, find a local beauty school that offers free or discounted haircuts.

▶ For men who choose to have facial hair, is important that facial hair be groomed and trimmed.

▶ Fresh breath during the interview is critical. Teeth should be brushed prior to the interview. Carry breath mints and use them before the interview as needed. Eating a small amount of food prior to the interview may also help maintain fresh breath by controlling unchecked stomach activity, but select mild foods that do not contribute to breath issues.

▶ Use deodorant. Avoid perfumes and scents.

▶ Appearance of fingernails can convey a professional image for both men and women. If money for manicures is a concern, see whether a local beauty school in the area offers free or discounted manicures. If fingernail polish is worn, it should be clear or a soft, neutral color.

▶ If you have body piercings or tattoos, remove any visible piercings and cover your tattoos to the extent possible.

CLOTHING FOR THE INTERVIEW

Preparing for an interview and selecting clothing should be done as soon as the interview has been scheduled. Having at least two interviewing outfits is important. By keeping both outfits clean and ready, you will be prepared for any potential accidents that may occur. If the interviewing outfits have not been worn for a while, try each outfit prior to the interview day to make sure it fits properly. Dry clean or wash items as needed, and complete any repairs such as missing buttons and frayed cuffs (Newberger, 2010). Take care of other considerations prior to the interview, such as ensuring that shoes are polished and briefcase and/or purse is cleaned, polished, and well organized. If a winter coat will be needed, make sure that it is clean and ready to be worn.

Men's and women's clothing suggestions for interview attire are as follows (Brookhaven College Career Development Center, n.d.; King's College Career Planning and Placement Office, n.d.).

Men

- Suits are the most preferred outfit for interviewing. Common colors for suits are navy, brown, or shades of gray. Black is acceptable, but some may find it too dark or gloomy. Most professionals indicate that a two-piece suit is most appropriate.

- Shirts should always be long sleeved and be of solid colors: light blue, cream, or white. The fabric typically preferred is either a cotton-polyester blend or 100% cotton. Shirts must be clean and lightly starched.

- Tie colors should complement or blend with the overall outfit. The preferred fabric is 100% silk with a simple pattern. Once tied, the tie should have a small knot and extend down to the trouser belt. The acceptable width of ties is usually between 2¾ inches and 3½ inches. Bow ties should be avoided.

- Shoes should be well polished and in good condition, with no apparent scuff marks or other flaws. Black, brown, or burgundy leather shoes work best with business suits. Socks should be dark, complement the suit, and be of calf length so that skin is not revealed when a man is sitting down and crossing his legs.

- Accessories such as belts should be selected to complement the shoes being worn. Jewelry should be minimal and typically includes only items such as a wedding band, tie tack, watch, and cuff links. No earrings or other facial piercing rings should be worn to the interview. No accessories or clothing should have any words or images that indicate personal beliefs, political views, or product advertisements. Tattoos should be covered

Digital Vision/Getty Images

Well-selected interview attire for men includes a neutral color two-piece suit, solid color shirt in a neutral color, tie in complementary color, polished shoes, and minimal jewelry. Hair and nails should be well groomed. Cover tattoos and remove any body jewelry from piercings.

6

when possible. Carry a leather briefcase that is in good condition. Make sure all of these items present a professional image.

Women

Jose Luis Pelaez/Iconica/Getty Images

Well-selected interview attire for women includes a neutral color, two-piece suit; a solid color blouse without added frills; polished neutral color pumps; neutral color hose; and accessories that complement the shoes.

▶ Skirt suits are the recommended attire for women for an interview. Dresses are acceptable but are less appropriate than a suit. If a dress is worn, then a matching jacket is highly recommended. Casual slacks should never be worn unless research of the company has indicated otherwise. Color choices for suits are typically beige, charcoal, gray, black, or navy blue. Skirts of knee length or 2 inches above the knee are recommended, but skirt length may be selected according to body type.

▶ Blouses in solid colors that complement the skirt should be selected. White or cream is recommended. Styles chosen should be selected to complement one's body type. Avoid blouses with front frills or lace and plunging necklines.

▶ Generally, basic pumps with low or medium heels work best. Shoes should be polished and in good condition. Colors that typically coordinate well with women's business suits include solid black, brown, navy, taupe, and burgundy. Panty hose must be new or in excellent condition and fit well to avoid any bagging at the ankles. Carry an extra pair just in case of an emergency. A neutral color that matches your skin tone is best.

▶ Accessories such as belts should be selected to complement or match the shoes being worn. Carry a briefcase rather than a purse. Carry a small, professional-appearing purse if you do not have an acceptable briefcase. Do not carry both. Make sure the

6

success steps for women's dressing

- Select a neutral color, two-piece suit with a skirt of appropriate style for your body type.
- Choose a suit over a dress. If a dress is worn, a jacket should be added.
- Select a solid color blouse without added frills. Avoid plunging necklines.
- Wear polished, neutral color pumps with a low to medium heel.
- Wear neutral color hose.
- Select accessories that complement the shoes.
- A briefcase is preferred to a purse. Do not carry both a briefcase and a purse.
- Select make-up that complements your skin tone and features but does not overwhelm.

briefcase appearance and its contents, such as pen and paper, present a professional image. Jewelry should be minimal and should only include items such as a wedding or engagement ring, necklace, earrings, bracelet, and watch. No more than one ring per hand should be worn. Earrings should not be dangly but close to the ear and should complement the entire outfit. No more than one set of earrings should be worn. Eyebrow or any other facial piercing jewelry should be removed. No piece of jewelry worn should draw too much attention.

▌ Make-up should be worn but should complement your skin tone rather than overwhelm your natural appearance. Dark eye shadows should be avoided. If nail polish is worn, it should be a subtle tone, such as pale pink or a clear gloss.

SELF-ASSESSMENT QUESTIONS

- What clothing do you own now that is appropriate for professional attire?
- What more can you learn about your skin tone and body type that might help enhance your appearance?

? CRITICAL THINKING QUESTION

▌ What is your reaction to the following statement? "It isn't the clothes that make a person.

6

apply it

Interview a Professional

GOAL: To develop further appreciation of what is entailed in dressing for success

STEP 1: Contact a professional in your field and arrange an interview. The purpose of the interview is to discuss the type of dress most appropriate for the profession.

STEP 2: For the interview, dress in clothing you believe is appropriate for interviewing with this individual. During the interview, ask the professional to critique your choice of dress and to offer suggestions for improvement.

STEP 3: Write a brief report on what you learned. Set goals for developing your professional wardrobe.

BUILDING A PROFESSIONAL WARDROBE ON A BUDGET

Often, college students find themselves without much additional cash. Consequently, budgeting for the eventual purchase of professional outfits should begin as soon as possible.

The Department of Apparel, Merchandising, Design, and Textiles at Washington State University (n.d.) makes the following suggestions for dressing professionally on a tight budget:

- Don't wait until the last minute to start looking for the outfits you need to purchase. Because you are on a tight budget, finding the best clothes you can get for your money may take some time. Take your time and make wise purchases.

- Keep in mind that you are not just purchasing these outfits for the interview but that these two outfits may need to serve you until you receive your first paycheck. Because of this, make sure the outfits can be mixed and matched to make a variety of outfits. Purchasing outfits with interchangeable components expands your possibilities and maximizes your wardrobe budget.

- Select a neutral tone such as black, dark gray, or navy around which to build your wardrobe. You can also choose contemporary colors such as pearl gray, steel blue, camel, and celery. When selecting colors, pay attention to those that best suit your skin tone.

- Do not overlook the important purchases of appropriate accessories and shoes. Budget these items into your overall plan.

- Purchase items that are washable to avoid dry-cleaning expenses.

- If travel may be required for the interview and/or job, select clothing that is less likely to wrinkle.

- Although you are on a budget, do not cut corners when it comes to quality. Invest in clothing that is well made, of durable fabric, and of a classic design that is less likely to go out of style with the next clothing trend.

- Consider thrift shops when necessary. Often, thrift stores have merchandise that was worn minimally by executives and businesspeople. Look for good name brands that offer quality. Inspect pieces for tears, frayed areas, and other signs of wear before purchasing. Check fabric for resistance to wrinkling by squeezing it in your hand.

> ## success steps for professional dressing on a budget
>
> - Begin budgeting early for your professional wardrobe.
> - Use the mix-and-match approach to stretch your wardrobe dollar.
> - Build your wardrobe around a neutral color base and add stylish, yet professional, colors to your base.
> - Shop for quality rather than quantity.
> - Buy washable fabrics to minimize dry-cleaning expenses.
> - Look for good-quality clothes in second-hand stores.
> - Seek the advice of an experienced and successful professional dresser.

▶ Finally, when in doubt, ask for help. Take someone shopping with you. This individual should be someone who has demonstrated the ability to dress professionally and whom you trust to help select the best items for your professional wardrobe.

DRESSING FOR CASUAL FRIDAYS

Once you start working at your new job, you may find that you have an opportunity to "dress down" one day a week. Many companies have instituted a "Casual Friday" dress policy. In general, this means dressing down a notch on Fridays from whatever the dress code of the company is typically. So, if a suit and tie is the norm, Casual Friday attire is likely dress slacks and a long-sleeved collared shirt. For other companies, Casual Friday might mean jeans and a t-shirt. Be sure to check with your company's human resources department to determine if there is such a policy and what the dress code is for that day. Remember, though, if you interview on a Casual Friday you should still dress in a professional manner as described in this chapter.

SELF-ASSESSMENT QUESTION

- What concerns might you have about affording new outfits? What can you do to alleviate these concerns?

6

CHAPTER SUMMARY

This chapter focused on professionalism and acceptable etiquette in the job search process. The importance of etiquette cannot be overstated, as employers appreciate high standards of behavior. The manners that you demonstrate are not only appealing to an employer, but also represent how you will treat clients in the future. In addition to emphasizing the importance of etiquette to your success in the job search and in the impression you make as a professional, general etiquette guidelines were provided. Then, etiquette requirements for specialized interview situations, including telephone, mealtime, and video chat interviews, were reviewed.

This chapter also examined the elements of dressing for success in your job search. Generally accepted standards of professional dress for interviews were also provided, as well as guidelines for accessorizing and attending to personal care issues. You also received suggestions for developing a professional wardrobe on a budget. Finally, you were introduced to the concept of dressing for Casual Fridays.

POINTS TO KEEP IN MIND

In this chapter, several main points were discussed in detail:

- Professional socialization is the process by which you will adopt the values and attitudes of your profession.
- Professionalism should be demonstrated during the job search process as well as on the job.
- Employers seek technically qualified individuals who also demonstrate good manners.
- Demonstrating phone etiquette is an important element of the job search process.
- Phone interviews are just as important as in-person interviews and should be treated with as much care and attention.
- Interviews conducted on cell phones require specific etiquette and considerations.
- General table manners need to be followed during a mealtime interview.
- Your dress and grooming is important and is a critical factor to getting hired.
- Accepting that your personal appearance does make a difference and working on doing what is necessary to make a good impression will be what differentiates a successful individual from a less successful one.
- By paying attention to clothing and color selections, individuals can enhance their outward appearance and in turn feel more confident.

- The presentation of your skills and abilities is the focus of the interview and is what should be heard. Don't let your clothes be the focus of the conversation.
- Being neat and clean is just as important as wearing the appropriate interview clothing.
- Establish a budget while still in college in order to be prepared to purchase the wardrobe items needed to dress for success.

CHECK YOUR UNDERSTANDING

Visit www.cengagebrain.com to see how well you have mastered the material in Chapter 6.

SUGGESTED ITEMS FOR LEARNING PORTFOLIO

- Importance of Proper Etiquette: This activity will familiarize you with the importance placed by employers on appropriate etiquette in the job search.
- Phone Interview Role-Play: This activity will give you an opportunity to practice telephone interview skills.
- Mealtime Interviewing: This activity will help you develop effective mealtime interview skills.
- Dressing for Success Research: This activity will develop your understanding of dress that is appropriate in your field.
- Interview a Professional: Interviewing a professional will increase your awareness of dress expectations in your field.

REFERENCES

The American Occupational Therapy Association (AOTA). (2010). Retrieved May 8, 2013, from http://www.aota.org/Consumers/Ethics/39880.aspx

Brookhaven College, Career Development Center. (n.d.). Dressing for the interview. Retrieved May 8, 2013, from http://www.brookhaven college.edu/pdf/careerctr/interviewattire.pdf

The Career Journal. (n.d.). Nine etiquette tips for job seekers. Retrieved May 8, 2013, from http://www.webco.cc/Interviewing%

6

20Articles/Nine%20Etiquette%20Tips%20For%20Job %20Seekers.pdf

Career Services Virginia Tech. (2013). Interview appearance and attire. Retrieved May 8, 2013, from http://www.career.vt.edu/interviewing /interviewappearance.html

The Center for Professional Excellence at York College of Pennsylvania (2012). *2012 Professionalism in the Workplace Study.* Retrieved May 22, 2013, from http://www.ycp.edu/media/yorkwebsite/cpe/2012 -Professionalism-in-the-Workplace-Study.pdf

Crawford Hentz, M. (n.d.[a]). Phone interview etiquette can propel you to the next step in the hiring process. Quintessential Careers. Retrieved May 8, 2013, from http://www.quintcareers.com/ phone_interview_etiquette.html

Crawford Hentz, M. (n.d.[b]). Phone interviewing do's and don'ts. Quintes-sential Careers. Retrieved May 8, 2013, from http://www.quintcareers .com/phone_interviewing-dos-donts.html

Deal, T. E., & Kennedy, A. A. (2000). *Corporate cultures: The rites and rituals of corporate life.* New York, New York: Basic Books.

King's College, Career Planning and Placement Office. (n.d.). Tips on interviewing. Retrieved May 8, 2013, from http://www2.kings.edu /academics/careerplanning/interv2.htm

Newberger, N. (2010). Dress for success. Retrieved May 8, 2013, from http://www.editionduo.com/display_article.php?id=519915

Pitney, W. A. (2002, July–Sept.). The professional socialization of certified athletic trainers in high school settings: A grounded theory investiga-tion [Electronic version]. U.S. Library of Medicine. Retrieved May 8, 2013, from http://www.ncbi.nlm.nih.gov/pubmed/12937587

Teschendorf, B., & Nemshick, M. (2001). Faculty roles in professional socialization [Electronic version]. *Journal of Physical Therapy Education,* Spring, 2001. Retrieved May 8, 2013, from http://www.questia.com /library/1P3-72022190/faculty-roles-in-professional-socialization

Washington State University, Department of Apparel, Merchandising, Design and Textiles. (n.d.). Dressing on a tight budget. Retrieved May 8, 2013, from http://amdt.wsu.edu/research/dti/Budget.html

Wisconsin Department of Workforce Development. (2010). Grooming for employment. Retrieved May 8, 2013, from http://www.dwd.state .wi.us/dwd/publications/dwsj/pdf/detj_4814_p.pdf

Yoakum, J. (2009). Formality, professionalism in your job search—some easliy overloooked items. Retrieved May 8, 2013, from http:// jimsbusinessblog.wordpress.com/2009/07/11/formality-professionalism -in-your-job-search-some-easliy-overloooked-items/

part 3

The Art of
the Interview

Part III of *100% Job Search Success* focuses on interviewing
success, the follow-up to interviewing, and entering the workforce.

Chapter 7: Successful Interviewing prepares you
with the foundation for preparing for and participating
effectively in a job interview.

Chapter 8: After the Interview discusses techniques
for interview follow-up, the elements of job negotiation, and
job rejection as an expected part of the job search.

Chapter 9: Professionalism in the Workplace
explores expected professional behaviors of employees as
they enter or re-enter the workforce.

Successful Interviewing

LEARNING OBJECTIVES

By the end of this chapter, you will achieve the following objectives:

▶ Explain the types of questions that can be asked in a job interview.

▶ Describe three types of interviews.

▶ Review types of interview questions.

▶ Discuss what makes an interview question illegal and explain appropriate responses to these types of questions.

▶ Explain accepted standards of interviewing.

▶ Discuss methods used to calm nerves before and during an interview.

▶ Define *nonverbal behavior* and provide examples of positive and negative nonverbal behavior in an interview.

▶ Discuss how to address your weaknesses or negatives in the interview.

▶ Demonstrate the ability to find sample interview questions and create acceptable answers to each.

▶ Practice interviewing skills by participating in a mock interview.

BE IN THE KNOW

That's Outrageous!

Recently, Careerbuilder.com conducted a survey of over 2,400 hiring managers, asking them about mistakes that candidates make when interviewing for a position. The following are some of the most outrageous blunders that hiring managers encountered (and they are all true!).

- Candidate provided a detailed listing of how previous employer made him mad.
- Candidate hugged hiring manager at the end of the interview.
- Candidate ate all the candy from the candy bowl while trying to answer questions.
- Candidate constantly bad-mouthed spouse.
- Candidate blew her nose and lined up the used tissues on the table in front of her.
- Candidate brought a copy of a college diploma with the original name obviously covered up and the candidate's name added.
- Candidate wore a hat that said "take this job and shove it."
- Candidate talked about how an affair cost him a previous job.
- Candidate threw his beer can in the outside trashcan before coming into the reception office.
- Candidate had a friend come in and ask "HOW MUCH LONGER?" (Careerbuilder.com 2011).

These are obviously extreme examples of what not to do during an interview. Nonetheless, it is important that you understand the best strategies to employ during an interview so that you get that all-important job. Read on!

 ## PREPARING FOR THE INTERVIEW

It is important to begin preparing for the interview as soon as it has been scheduled. Areas that require consideration when preparing for an interview include the following:

- Update your resumé and reference list as needed and make copies to take to the interview.
- Prepare and organize your portfolio with anything that is related to the job. Refer to Chapter 5 for information on portfolio content and organization.
- Make sure what you will wear has been purchased and is clean and ready. Chapter 6 provided a detailed discussion regarding appropriate interview attire.
- Purchase any necessary pens, paper, or other materials that may be needed for the interview.

7

▸ Consult the company's or a map web site to determine the best way to get to the interview location.

Another aspect of preparing for the interview includes conducting research on the company. Employers expect applicants for a position have taken the time to research the company and what the job entails. The Internet can usually provide useful information. Locate the company's web site and familiarize yourself with the company's current projects, events, and issues. A company's annual report can also provide significant information. If you still need information beyond the company's web site, outside reviews may be helpful. Private companies usually provide less information than public companies. Good sources for information on private companies include Forbes Largest Private Companies list and the Inc. 500, which is a list of America's fastest-growing privately held companies. For public companies, good sources of information can be found at Business Week Online: Company Research, and Hoovers Online (Hansen, n.d.[c]).

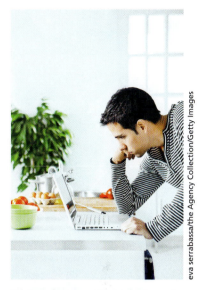

The Internet is an effective resource for conducting industry research related to your job search.

In addition to conducting research, applicants need to fully understand what skills and abilities they are bringing to the employer. They also need to be able to specifically relate their skills to the requirements of the job. Employers want to know that the applicant they choose is the best fit for the required tasks of the job.

The best way to prepare for an interview:

▸ Obtain and review the job description of the position for which you are applying. If possible, obtain a copy of the job description prior to the interview. If this is not possible,

apply it

Researching Companies

GOAL: To develop more information regarding companies of interest

STEP 1: Research three companies for which you might like to work.

STEP 2: From the information that you find, prepare a brief report of your findings. Are you still interested now that you know more about the company? Why or why not? What web sites were used?

STEP 3: Share your information with the class.

STEP 4: Consider placing this company information in your Learning Portfolio.

7

you may be able to obtain a description of a job that is similar enough to provide you information about the tasks and responsibilities that are desired for the job. See Figure 7-1 for an example of a job description.

▶ Be clear about the knowledge that is necessary to do the job. Note the other skills and personal qualities that may be required or desired.

Job Description

Position: Medical Assistant
Reports to: Physician/Nurses/Office Manager

Responsibilities:

The MA is responsible for the flow of patients through the office. Serves as a liaison between the patient and the physician and assists in ensuring quality patient care. Works directly with the physician and nurses in providing care to patients. Works with other ancillary departments such as radiology and lab in arranging testing and procedures for patients.

Duties include:

1. Obtains information regarding the patient's past history and current illness.
2. Takes and records vital signs of the patient including weight, temperature, pulse rate, respiration, and blood pressure.
3. Escorts patients to exam rooms and prepares patients for exams.
4. Assists physician with the treatment of the patient.
5. Assists the physicians in procuring lab samples and requisitions.
6. Schedules appointments for all referred cases.
7. Assists other office staff, when necessary, in making appointments, calling patients, locating charts, and filling reports in the medical chart.
8. Manages medical and drug supply inventory, Originates orders as needed.
9. Maintains sample supply closet.
10. Keeps examining rooms clean and stocked.
11. Properly disposes of contaminated and disposable items.
12. Assists in retrieving past medical records for patients as required for the patient's office visit.
13. Retrieves labs, x-rays, and other test results. Pulls appropriate patient chart and attaches report(s) to the file for physician viewing.
14. Conducts routine lab work and EKG's as ordered by the physician.
15. Performs other duties as assigned by the physician/office manager.

Job requirements:

Graduation from an accredited MA program and current certification.
Enjoy working with people in a positive productive environment.
Possess the verbal ability to understand patient medical records, physician orders and medication orders, to be communicative with the patient and hospital staff.
Possess the ability to deal tactfully and effectively with patients, parents, and other employees, hospital staff, and the physician.

Figure 7-1   A job description outlines the responsibilities and expectations associated with a position. Doing an excellent job and advancing in your field often requires going above and beyond the expectations listed on the job description.

success steps for preparing for an interview

- Review a job description, if possible. If a job description is not available, find out as much as you can about the position on the company's web site or from their human resources department.
- Be familiar with the knowledge you will need to do the job.
- Find out what kind of interview will be conducted, if possible.
- Anticipate questions that might be asked and how you would answer them.
- Prepare questions to ask the employer.

▶ If possible, discover what type of interview will be conducted. For instance, will it be a group interview, phone interview, online interview, or behavioral interview? Is the interview to take place over lunch or dinner?

▶ Anticipate the questions that may be asked and prepare answers in advance.

▶ Prepare questions that should be asked of the employer.

STRATEGIES FOR SUCCESSFUL INTERVIEWING

A successful interview doesn't "just happen." In order to ensure that your interviews go well and hopefully land you that job, consider the following strategies.

CASE IN POINT: THEY SAY FIRST IMPRESSIONS . . .

Read the scenario below. Then, in groups or as a class, answer the questions at the end.

As the company's Director of Human Resources, Julie spends much of her time interviewing applicants for various job openings. Julie's secretary just called her to tell her that the next applicant, Susan Edge, had arrived. Upon arriving in the lobby to meet Susan, Julie began her assessment of the applicant. Sitting in the lobby was a woman with a navy suit, pale pink blouse, and matching navy

continued

7

continued

blue shoes. Beside her was an attractive leather briefcase. As Julie approached, the woman rose and introduced herself as Susan Edge. Julie noticed that Susan waited until Julie extended her hand in order to receive a handshake. After the introductions, Julie escorted Susan back to her office. Upon entering the office, Susan waited to be offered a chair and then both Julie and Susan sat for the interview. Prior to the first question, Susan asked Julie if it would be acceptable for her to take notes during the interview. The interview then began.

- What did Susan do to help Julie begin to form opinions about her professionalism and abilities?
- How in this brief scenario did Susan demonstrate her abilities as a detail-oriented individual?
- What kind of impression did Susan make by waiting to accept Julie's handshake and waiting to be asked to sit?
- If Susan had extended her hand first or had sat before being offered a chair, what impressions, if any, might have been made? Should these actions affect Julie's overall opinion of Susan?

INTERVIEW LOGISTICS

Preparing for the interview will significantly help in the overall success of the experience. In addition to considering questions and your answers, what you will wear, and the materials you need for the interview, a few other simple rules should be followed for a successful interviewing experience. The following suggestions for a successful interview can help reduce stress and increase confidence (Hansen, n.d.[b]):

- Make sure you know how to get to the interview. If necessary, do a dry run a day or two before the interview to make sure you know how long it will take to get there. Arriving at least 10 to 15 minutes ahead of the scheduled interview is suggested; arriving late to an interview is unacceptable. If a late arrival is unavoidable due to an emergency, call the company to alert the employer to the situation. Remember that a late arrival for any reason will make a poor impression. Always call as far in advance as possible if you must cancel the appointment. Do not simply fail to show up for the interview. If this occurs, you not only ruin your chances for getting the job, but your actions show disrespect for the employer's time, as the time could have been used for interviewing someone else. Remember, too, that the professional world is a small one and word does travel. Your actions toward one employer may influence your chances with another.

▶ On the day of the interview, allow extra time for preparing and driving to the interview site. Allow for traffic and other possible delays, including inclement weather.

▶ The night before the interview, prepare your briefcase with all necessary items, such as copies of your resumé, reference list, and portfolio. Take two or three pens and some paper. Consider all necessary items/information you may be required to supply the employer. For example, having the names and addresses of references might be beneficial should the interviewer request them.

▶ Take your cell phone (or other communications device) for any last-minute calls you might need to make or to use in the event of an emergency. However, be sure to turn it off when you arrive at the interview.

▶ As you arrive for your interview, present a calm and organized demeanor. If you have prepared effectively and allowed ample time, you will avoid arriving breathless and harried. Arrive with a pleasant friendly smile, greet the receptionist with professionalism, and offer your first and last name. Establish good eye contact as you speak. Remember that first impressions can make a difference.

▶ If a job application is presented to you, fill it out neatly and provide correct and accurate details as required.

7

success steps for effective participation in an interview

- Familiarize yourself with the location of the interview before the actual date.
- On the day of the interview, allow extra time for preparing and arriving at the site.

continued

continued

- Prepare your briefcase with the necessary items ahead of time.
- Take your cell phone. Be sure to turn it off when you arrive.
- Enter the interview setting with a calm and organized demeanor.
- Complete any paperwork that is requested.

SUCCESSFUL INTERVIEWING TECHNIQUES

The purpose of an interview is not necessarily to get a job. Most of the time the purpose of the interview is to provide more information to the applicant and employer to determine whether the fit is right. Often, an applicant really does not know whether the job is right for him or her until the interview has taken place. Sometimes during the interview, either one or both of the parties may conclude that the job is not a good fit. This does not mean that the interview was a failure. The interview is only a failure if the applicant neither presented him- or herself professionally nor expressed his or her skills and abilities clearly enough for the employer to choose the right candidate for the job.

Once the interview begins, it is important to remain calm and confident. The preparation that has been done prior to the interview supports a relaxed and effective presentation. The following are some suggestions to help make the interviewing experience more positive (Bellevue University Career Services, n.d.; Hansen, n.d.[c]):

- Not all individuals are perfect at the job of interviewing. If your interviewer is less than effective, it is your job as the applicant to remain courteous and answer the questions as asked. Provide thorough and effective information. Having difficulty with an individual interviewer does not necessarily mean you will not get the job. Remain professional and do not run the risk of ruining your chances due to an interviewer's inadequacies.

- Turn off all cell phones and pagers prior to entering the interview.

- Do not allow family members, children, friends, or other individuals to accompany you to an interview.

- Request a cup of water prior to the beginning of the interview. Nerves often create dry mouth. Do not chew gum or suck on a breath mint during the interview. Avoid yawning, as it can indicate boredom.

▶ Answer each question with consideration and care. Some questions may not seem as important as others, but the interviewer probably has good reason for asking each one.

▶ Prior to answering a question, it is acceptable to pause and make sure your answer is well thought out. Moments of silence are reasonable in order to prepare a thoughtful response. Demonstrating the ability to reflect on and think through an answer shows the ability to consider relevant issues and attend to details.

▶ Avoid making jokes and being overly friendly with the interviewer. You want to appear professional.

▶ Use good grammar. Avoid pausing words such as *um* or *uh*. Taking a moment to reflect and plan what to say is preferable.

▶ Speak up. Soft-spoken individuals may be seen as lacking confidence.

▶ Demonstrate effective listening skills. Never interrupt the interviewer. Effective listening will communicate a desirable workplace skill and enable you to answer the question more appropriately.

▶ Clarify questions as needed. It is appropriate to ask questions if you do not understand something. Clarifying questions will allow you to provide more effective and appropriate answers.

▶ Be positive about your experiences and achievements, but avoid exaggerating or embellishing the truth. Doing so will catch up with you later.

▶ When responding to questions, be as clear and succinct as possible. Whenever possible, answer questions with more than just a "yes" or "no." Provide examples when possible to further explain answers, including portfolio pieces, as applicable, but avoid rambling.

▶ Avoid topics such as religion and politics. If the interviewer brings up any controversial topics, remain vague and non-committal. It is inappropriate to share your opinion.

▶ When answering questions, do not hesitate to demonstrate the knowledge you have gained about the company through your research. Employers will appreciate your efforts. Avoid being cocky about your knowledge, which may be perceived as showing off.

7

▶ Avoid discussion of your personal life.

▶ Avoid criticizing a former employer or colleague. If you experienced difficulties or are asked about a difficult time, describe the situation as a positive learning experience. Accept responsibility that is yours and describe how you would change for the better.

▶ Avoid overuse of hand gestures. If this is a natural inclination, then try folding your hands together on your lap. This will also help those who have a tendency to chew their nails (Dress for Success, n.d.).

▶ If you trip or accidentally knock something over, do not panic. Showing you can handle these types of incidents demonstrates that you handle pressure well (Dress for Success, n.d.).

▶ Always have some questions written down that you want to ask the employer. By asking questions you demonstrate your interest and intelligence.

▶ Focus on what you offer the company and how your abilities meet company needs. "Always keep the focus on what you can do for the company; the interviewer is most concerned with your ability to do the job and benefit the company, not with the company's ability to meet your expectations" (Bellevue University Career Services, n.d., "Selling Yourself during the Interview").

▶ Avoid appearing desperate for the job. The employer may begin to wonder why you have not been hired anywhere.

▶ Do not bring up salary and benefits. Salary negotiation will be covered in detail in Chapter 8. Bellevue University Career Services (n.d.) makes the following suggestions regarding salary and benefit discussions:

• Salary is typically discussed in later interviews. Wait for the employer to raise the issue of salary and benefits. After the issue is mentioned, it is appropriate to ask questions.

• Wait until the interviewer offers a salary figure before stating your expectations. If you are asked to identify an amount, ask what the salary range is for the position. If you have a minimum acceptable salary figure, it is acceptable to state it, but realize that doing so may eliminate you from consideration if the amount is not acceptable to the employer.

• Keep in mind that benefits also contribute to the total package. Benefit packages that include health and life insurance, retirement plans, and other features are costly and can add significant value to your salary.

▶ If you are interested in the job at the end of the interview, tell the interviewer. Ask about the next step in the hiring process, to demonstrate interest. Find out when you should expect to hear from the employer.

▶ Obtain the name and title of the interviewer at the end of the interview. Get a business card if possible. It is appropriate (and important!) to send the interviewer a thank-you note as follow-up to the interview.

▶ After you have left the company, spend a few minutes in your car or at a quiet place taking notes on your experience. Jot down your thoughts and further questions that may need researching.

It is difficult to totally fail in an interview. Employers typically are understanding about the stress that applicants are experiencing, and many employers do their best to alleviate applicants' anxieties.

Kathleen Brooks
432 East Brooks Avenue
Denver, CO 80000

November 20, 2013

Ms. Christina Chung
Human Resources Director
Everett Technologies
10067 Mountain View Road
Broomfield, CO 82222

Dear Ms. Chung:

Thank you for taking the time yesterday to meet with me regarding the office manager position at Everett Technologies. The programs we discussed seem to be leading the company in exciting new directions. I believe that my experience with and knowledge of streamlining systems and tracking data would greatly facilitate your implementation of these new programs. In addition, the positive relationships I have developed with office staff in the past have provided me with a foundation for working effectively with diverse individuals in the office setting.

Everett Technologies' innovative and forward thinking perspective is impressive and I believe I could contribute significantly to your growth. I would appreciate your serious consideration of my candidacy for the office manager position.

Thank you again for the opportunity to meet with you and learn about your company. I look forward to hearing from you.
Sincerely,

Kathleen Brooks

Figure 7-2 An effective thank-you letter acknowledges the employer's time spent and the information provided as well as highlights your skills and positive perceptions of the position and organization.

success steps for interviewing successfully

- Remain courteous under all circumstances and answer the questions as asked.
- Turn off all cell phones and pagers prior to the interview.
- Do not allow family members, children, or friends to attend the interview.
- Request a cup of water prior to the beginning of the interview in the event your mouth becomes dry.
- Answer each question with consideration and care.
- Prior to answering a question, it is acceptable to pause.
- Avoid making jokes and being overly friendly with the interviewer.
- Use good grammar. Avoid pausing words such as *um* or *uh*.
- Speak up to avoid being seen as lacking confidence.
- Demonstrate effective listening skills. Never interrupt the interviewer.
- Clarify questions as needed.
- Be positive about your experiences and achievements, but avoid exaggerating.
- When responding to questions, be as clear and succinct as possible.
- Avoid topics such as religion and politics.
- When answering questions, do not hesitate to demonstrate the knowledge you have gained about the company through research.
- Avoid discussion of your personal life.
- Avoid criticizing a former employer or colleague.
- Avoid overuse of hand gestures.
- If you trip or accidentally knock something over, handle the situation with grace and poise.
- Always have some questions written down to ask the employer.
- Focus on what you offer the company and how your abilities meet company needs.
- Avoid appearing desperate for the job.
- Do not bring up salary and benefits.
- If you are interested in the job at the end of the interview, tell the interviewer.
- Obtain the name and title of the interviewer at the end of the interview so that you can send a thank-you note.
- After you have left the company, spend a few minutes in your car or at a quiet place to record notes about your experience.

7

Addressing Your Weaknesses

Addressing your weaknesses can be one of the most challenging aspects of the interview. Interviewers *love* to ask the "what are your weaknesses?" question in an attempt to derail you from what might be an otherwise successful interview. Knowing that honesty is essential, many struggle with how to present weaknesses in the most positive light. Career coaches recommend that you be prepared for this inevitable question. The following are some suggested "dos and don'ts" for addressing weaknesses during a job interview:

▶ **Do be honest.** If you are not honest with your answer, it may well come back to haunt you. Do not lose sight of the fact that employers will check your references, academic record, and employment history. Owning up to your weaknesses is a sign of maturity and professionalism. The interviewer will appreciate your forthrightness and perceive that as a valued trait in you.

▶ **Do explain how you are working to improve your weaknesses.** For example, let's say you are shy, especially in larger groups. You can address working to improve your shyness by saying that you are taking classes on public speaking or that you are volunteering at a local food bank. The important point to get across to the interviewer is that not only do you recognize your weakness, you are addressing it and are continuing to work to turn it into a strength.

▶ **Don't say that you don't have weaknesses.** Talk about being conceited! Everyone, including your interviewer, has weaknesses. Saying that you don't have any is not only a bold-faced lie, it's an insult to the interviewer. No employer is ever going to hire you because you don't have any weaknesses. They know it, and you should own up to them.

▶ **Do not turn a strength into a weakness.** Saying that you are too detail-oriented, for example, could cost you the job if in fact the position calls for you to be very detailed in your work. This approach also shows that you have little capacity for self-assessment or learning (Lewis, 2012).

Poor performance in an interview can be attributed to a variety of reasons. By practicing interviewing skills and gaining confidence in your abilities, you will become more successful in the interviewing process.

SELF-ASSESSMENT QUESTION

• What scares you or makes you nervous about interviewing? How can you overcome these fears?

7

❓ CRITICAL THINKING QUESTION

▶ If you lack experience in the job you are applying for, how can you address this weakness in a positive light?

apply it

Mock Interviews

GOAL: To demonstrate, in a mock interview, the ability to perform

STEP 1: Select a partner with whom you will complete this activity.

STEP 2: For the first round, one of you will act as the employer and the other as the job applicant. Using the questions developed in the Writing Interview Questions and Answers activity, ask and answer questions. Understand the importance of treating this exercise with as much sincerity and seriousness as you would an employment interview. After one of you has played the role of the employer and the other the applicant, switch roles and repeat the exercise.

STEP 3: After the exercise, reconvene as a class and discuss what was learned in the mock interviews, what areas were difficult, and how you might continue to improve.

DEALING WITH FEELINGS OF NERVOUSNESS

Most individuals feel nervous at interviews. The following are a few suggestions to help you calm feelings of apprehension, based on Bowman (n.d.).

▶ **Have realistic expectations.** Avoid elevating the position to your "dream job" or, conversely, telling yourself that you will never land the job. Keep the job prospect in perspective and focus on preparing for and doing your best in the interview.

▶ **Know what you bring to the job.** Establish a clear relationship between your experience and skills and the requirements of the job. Be able to articulate this relationship clearly and directly.

▶ **Prepare.** Research the company, update your resumé and portfolio, and ready your wardrobe. Thorough preparation and a working knowledge of your resumé, the company, and the position can increase your confidence and reduce anxiety.

▶ **Take care of yourself.** Pay attention to your physical well-being. Get ample rest the night before your interview, eat a healthy and well-balanced meal beforehand, and avoid foods that don't agree with you.

▶ **Familiarize yourself with the interview site**. In addition to ensuring that you will be on time for the interview, arriving early provides you with an opportunity to focus and center

> ### success steps for dealing with feelings of nervousness
>
> - Have realistic expectations.
> - Know what you bring to the job.
> - Prepare.
> - Take care of yourself.
> - Familiarize yourself with the interview site.

your energy. Getting a brief overview of your surroundings can reduce nervousness. A stop in the restroom to ensure that you look your best will also help you relax.

Some individuals perspire more when anxious. If this is the case for you, make sure you have put on fresh deodorant and powder. Wear clothing that allows your body to breathe. If the interview room is warm, ask whether it is acceptable to take off your jacket. It is better to be comfortable than dripping wet during the interview. Prior to shaking the interviewer's hands, wash your hands with hot water. This will eliminate or minimize sweaty and clammy palms.

The Santa Clara University Career Center (n.d., p. 1) suggests asking yourself the following questions to alleviate some of your anxieties by addressing fears objectively:

▶ What do I fear most about the interview situation? What is the worst thing that can happen?

▶ If I were giving advice to someone else in this situation, what would I tell him/her?

Nonverbal behaviors, such as eye contact and shaking hands, communicate as much about you as (perhaps more than) what you say.

THE IMPORTANCE OF NONVERBAL BEHAVIORS

An applicant's nonverbal behavior is just as important as the responses he or she gives to the interviewer's questions. During the interview, applicants need to be aware of what they might be communicating through their nonverbal behaviors. Nonverbal behaviors include your facial expressions, posture, and hand gestures. Examining and adjusting body language and appearance is critical to interview success and making a positive impression on the employer. The following

success steps for nonverbal communication during the interview

- Your posture is important. Sit upright in the chair, and relax and lean forward slightly to show your interest.
- Keep your hands loosely clasped in your lap or on the table and away from your face.
- Direct eye contact shows that you are actively listening.
- To show confidence, speak in a clear and controlled voice.

Javier Pierini/Getty Images

7

The purpose of the interview is to provide both the applicant and potential employer the opportunity to exchange information and determine whether the position and applicant are a good fit.

examples illustrate how positive body language can make a difference (Best-job-interview.com, 2013):

▸ Your posture is a giveaway as to your nervousness or a careless attitude. Make sure you sit upright in the chair, and relax and lean forward slightly to show your interest.

▸ What should you do with your hands? At a minimum, keep them loosely clasped in your lap or on the table. And keep your hands away from your face. Some body language interview experts believe that touching your nose or lips indicates that the candidate is lying.

▸ Direct eye contact shows that you are actively listening. When you are speaking, maintain eye contact for 10 seconds, experts say, then look away briefly before reestablishing eye contact.

▸ Your voice delivery counts as well. To show confidence, speak in a clear and controlled voice. Varying tone and pitch is important as well. Just don't overdo it so that you appear excited or emotional. And make sure that your tone is not apologetic or defensive.

TYPES OF INTERVIEWS

There are three types of interviews that you may come across as you complete your job search: traditional, behavioral, and situational. Each type of interview serves a specific purpose and each kind has particular ways of asking questions of the candidate.

TRADITIONAL INTERVIEWS

Traditional interviews are those with which you may be the most familiar. These types of interviews are generally one-on-one with either a human resources person or the hiring manager (and sometimes both people). Traditional interviewing can be considered "skills-based."

Hansen (n.d.[d]) suggests that with traditional interviews the interviewer is looking for the answers to three questions:

- Does the job seeker have the skills and abilities to perform the job?
- Does the job seeker possess the enthusiasm and work ethic that the employer expects?
- Will the job seeker be a team player and fit into the organization?

The success or failure of the interview rests on the candidate's aptitude for articulating answers to questions is often seen as being more important than the truthfulness or substance of the answers. Traditional interviewing questions are generally broad-based and open-ended.

BEHAVIORAL INTERVIEWS

Behavioral interviews are designed to go beyond the traditional skills-based interview. Also known as "competency-based" interviews, behavioral interviews delve into your character and personal traits by asking questions about your former behavior. Hiring managers seek to determine if those past behaviors will indicate future success at the company (Turner, n.d.). For example, an interviewer may ask a question such as "What is your typical way of dealing with conflict? Give me an example." (See sample behavioral interview questions later in this chapter.)

So how do you prepare for a behavioral interview? Joe Turner, a professional recruiter, advises crafting several 30- to 90-second stories that showcase the skills and abilities that you would bring to the position. Turner suggests that stories be developed in these areas:

- A crisis in your life or job and how you responded or recovered from it.
- A time where you functioned as part of a team and what your contribution was.
- A time in your career or job where you had to overcome stress.

7

▶ A time in your job where you provided successful leadership or a sense of direction.

▶ A failure that occurred in your job and how did you overcome it.

Your stories should be designed to grab the interviewer's attention, give him something to remember you by, and be as detailed as possible. As with any type of interview, practice your answers, and in this case stories, several times before the interview. Just remember to have a fresh delivery during the interview so as not to sound robotic (Turner, n.d.).

SITUATIONAL INTERVIEWS

Situational interviews are similar to behavioral interviews, but instead of asking questions about past behaviors, this type of interview seeks to reveal how you would respond to a hypothetical situation that you might find on the job. For example, the interviewer might ask, "What would you do if the priorities on a project you were working on changed suddenly?" (See sample situational interview questions later in this chapter.)

Situational interviews draw on a candidate's analytical and problem-solving skills and one's ability to react to a situation on short notice or with minimal preparation. If you have gone to the effort of creating stories as suggested in the Behavioral Interview section above, use those same stories to explain how you would solve the problem that is presented by turning your examples of what you did into what you would do in that situation (Hansen, n.d.[d]).

TYPES OF INTERVIEW QUESTIONS

As with types of interviews, there are different types of questions that you may be asked during an interview. Regardless of which types of questions you are asked, it is important that you fully prepare yourself for all question types ahead of time.

PREPARING FOR INTERVIEW QUESTIONS

Preparing for questions that may be asked during the interview takes time and thoughtful reflection. One way to anticipate questions that might be asked is to seek advice from an expert, such as career placement personnel at your school. Or research commonly asked interview questions on the Internet, using "interview questions" as your search term. Once you have examples of questions, consider recording well-thought-out

7

answers. Use the questions and answers to conduct the mock interview activity introduced later in this chapter with a friend, family member, or a professional in your chosen career. Have the "employer" ask questions to which you must appropriately respond. After the mock interview, ask the "employer" to evaluate how you conducted yourself and the answers that you provided. Be open to constructive criticism and repeat the mock interview as many times as necessary to improve in areas that are weak.

Depending on the company, more than one interviewer may attend the interview session. The purpose of a team interview is often to save both the employer's and the applicant's time. Although team interviews can be more challenging than the traditional one-on-one approach, it is important to mentally prepare for the possibility of a team interview. Caroselli (n.d.) suggests recognizing that team interviews are more stressful than traditional interviews and recommends making a connection with each interviewer and using various examples from your experience rather than repeating the same example. Be prepared for the chance of a team interview, as you may not be informed in advance that a team approach will be taken. As with traditional interview formats, practicing, researching the company, preparing intelligent questions, and listening effectively contribute to a less stressful and more successful team interview. In addition, seek the assistance of your career placement personnel and conduct research to familiarize yourself with team interviewing.

COMMON INTERVIEW QUESTIONS

Many of the questions below are used during a traditional job interview. Be prepared to answer any (or all) of the following common interview questions.

- ❱ Why should we hire you?
- ❱ Tell me about yourself.
- ❱ What can you tell us about our company?
- ❱ Where do you see yourself in five years?
- ❱ Why did you decide to seek a position in this company?
- ❱ What are your long-range career objectives?
- ❱ How would a good friend describe you?
- ❱ In what ways do you think you can make a contribution to this company?
- ❱ What makes you qualified for this position? (Hansen, n.d.[a]).

SELF-ASSESSMENT QUESTIONS

- What types of questions do you think you might find most challenging in an interview?
- What steps do you need to take to become more comfortable with these questions?

BEHAVIORAL INTERVIEW QUESTIONS

As you have learned, behavioral interview questions focus on past behaviors. The following is a sampling of behavioral questions that you may be asked during an interview.

- Describe a situation in which you were able to use persuasion to successfully convince someone to see things your way.
- Describe a time when you were faced with a stressful situation that demonstrated your coping skills.
- Give me a specific example of a time when you used good judgment and logic in solving a problem.
- Give me an example of a time when you set a goal and were able to meet or achieve it.
- Tell me about a time when you had to use your presentation skills to influence someone's opinion.
- Give me a specific example of a time when you had to conform to a policy with which you did not agree.
- Please discuss an important written document you were required to complete.
- Tell me about a time when you had to go above and beyond the call of duty in order to get a job done.
- Tell me about a time when you had too many things to do and you were required to prioritize your tasks.
- Give me an example of a time when you had to make a split second decision (Quintessential Careers, n.d.[a]).

SITUATIONAL INTERVIEW QUESTIONS

Quintessential Careers offers up the following sample situational interview questions:

- Who would you talk to if you discovered that a coworker was disclosing confidential information that should not be divulged?
- When would it be appropriate to bring in your supervisor while dealing with an angry customer?
- How would you attempt to make changes in the process if you felt a policy of your organization was hurting its members/workers?

7

▶ What would a good manager do to build team spirit?

▶ How would you organize the steps or methods you'd take to define/identify a vision for your team or your personal job function?

▶ How would you react if two teammates were embroiled in a conflict that kept the team from completing its task?

▶ You don't have the information you need to prioritize your projects. Your coworkers and supervisor are unavailable for you to ask for assistance. How do you handle the situation?

▶ As a supervisor, you've made an unpopular decision. What action would you take so that morale in the department is not negatively affected?

▶ In a team-leadership role, you discover that a team member has gone "over your head" to propose an idea or complain about an issue without talking to you first. How do you handle the situation?

▶ You been placed in charge of a project team for a new project. What are your first steps to get the team going and complete the project (Quintessential Careers, n.d.[b])?

ILLEGAL INTERVIEW QUESTIONS

There are some questions that employers cannot legally ask due to the nature of the questions. It is important for applicants to be aware of what these questions are and how to respond professionally to any such question that might be asked. Questions asked during an interview must pertain to the position and your ability to effectively perform tasks associated with it. The following are areas about which employers are prohibited from asking questions (Office of Resources Management, University of Albany, n.d.):

▶ Age

▶ Birthplace, nationality, ancestry or descent of applicant, applicant's spouse, or parents

▶ Marital or family status

▶ Gender, race, color

▶ Religion or religious days observed

▶ Membership in organizations associated with a particular race, religion, or ethic group.

▶ Information about arrests, disabilities, or health conditions unrelated to job performance. Employers *are* permitted to ask questions about an applicant's ability to perform a specific task that is related to the job. For example, an employer can ask you if you can lift 30 pounds if that is a requirement of the job. The employer is prohibited from asking you if you have any disabilities.

If the interviewer asks an illegal question, it was probably unintentional. As a job applicant, it is important to respond professionally to any question that appears to be illegal. If handled correctly, the interviewer will not be made to feel uncomfortable as the question is left unanswered. Here are a few options for responding to illegal questions, as recommended by the Student Involvement & Career Center at San Francisco State University (n.d.) "Tactful Answers to Illegal Interview Questions."

Option 1. Explore the meaning behind the question or its intent and respond to that meaning.

▶ For example, your response to "Where were you born?" might be, "If you are wondering about my status, I am authorized to work in the United States."

▶ Your response to a question about marital status or young children might be, "If you are concerned about my ability to travel, let me assure you that I am prepared to make all the necessary arrangements so that I can travel the amount of time you indicated is likely in this job."

Option 2. Ask about the relationship of the information to the job.

▶ For example, if asked about your place of birth: "I'm not sure what my place of birth has to do with my qualifications for this position." Wait for a response from the interviewer and see whether he or she can explain how this question connects to the job requirements. You can at this point choose to either answer the question or decline.

Option 3. Refuse to answer the question. However, with this approach you run the risk of coming across as uncooperative or confrontational. Avoid taking this tactic if at all possible.

Option 4. Answer the question to avoid confronting the interviewer and possibly hurting your chances of being hired.

7

? CRITICAL THINKING QUESTION

▶ What is your reaction to the following statement? "If an employer asks me a question that I do not want to answer, I will just tell the interviewer I am unable to answer the question."

apply it

Writing Interview Questions and Answers

GOAL: *To demonstrate the ability to write interview questions and provide appropriate answers*

STEP 1: Write at least 30 questions that you think may be asked in an interview. For each question, provide a response.

STEP 2: Ask your instructor to review the questions and answers and make suggestions for improvements.

STEP 3: Consider the career placement personnel at your school as an additional resource for this exercise.

STEP 4: Consider putting your questions and answers in your Learning Portfolio.

QUESTIONS TO ASK AN EMPLOYER DURING AN INTERVIEW

Although you will be answering many questions during your interview, an effective tool you can use to your benefit is to ask questions of your prospective employer. Take the time to write down carefully thought-out questions and bring them to the interview with you. Interviewers almost always build in time to allow for questions from the interviewee. Do not ask questions for the sake of asking questions, however. Any information that can be found through the Internet or other research about the company should not be asked.

Quintessential Careers (n.d.[c]) suggests the best questions to formulate and ask are those that are very specific about the employer. The following are some general questions that you can ask your interviewer, but only if they have not been answered during the course of the interview.

- Can you describe a typical day for someone in this position?
- What is the top priority of the person who accepts this job?
- What are the day-to-day expectations and responsibilities of this job?
- How will my leadership responsibilities and performance be measured? And by whom? How often?
- Can you describe the company's (or division's or department's) management style?

▶ Can you discuss your take on the company's corporate culture?

▶ How would you describe the company's values?

▶ How would you characterize the management philosophy of this organization? Of your department?

▶ Does the organization support ongoing training and education for employees to stay current in their fields?

▶ What do you think is the greatest opportunity facing the organization in the near future? The biggest threat?

▶ Why did you come to work here? What keeps you here?

▶ How is this department perceived within the organization?

▶ Is there a formal process for advancement within the organization?

▶ What are the traits and skills of people who are the most successful within the organization?

▶ What is the organization's policy on transfers to other divisions or other offices?

If you sense that your questions are bothering the interviewer or are taking up too much time, stop and allow the interview to wrap up.

CHAPTER SUMMARY

This chapter provided you with the foundation for preparing for and participating effectively in a job interview. Suggestions for preparing included updating your resumé and reference list, organizing your portfolio, and preparing responses to potential interview questions. You reviewed strategies for successful interviewing as well as methods for minimizing nervousness before and during the interview. The impact of nonverbal behaviors on the interview was emphasized. You learned ways to address your weaker areas during the interview and reviewed general behaviors that are likely to contribute to a less stressful and more successful interview. Additionally, you learned about the three types of interviews and associated specific interview questions tailored to each type of interview. Finally, strategies were given for diffusing illegal interview questions and examples were given of questions to ask the interviewer.

POINTS TO KEEP IN MIND

In this chapter, several main points were discussed in detail:

▶ Conducting research about the company where one will be interviewing is an important step to successful interviewing.

▶ Job applicants must be able to clearly and succinctly explain their strengths and abilities during the interview.

▶ There are three main types of interviews: traditional, behavioral, and situational.

▶ Different types of interview questions are asked based upon the type of interview being conducted.

▶ Conducting mock interviews as practice can substantially increase success in employment interviews.

▶ It is illegal to ask certain types of questions during an interview. The job applicant must be familiar with what constitutes illegal questions and how to professionally respond if such questions are asked.

▶ An applicant's nonverbal behavior is just as important as the responses given to the interviewer's questions.

▶ An interview is only a failure if the applicant fails to present himself or herself professionally and fails to express his or her skills and abilities clearly enough for the employer to choose the right candidate for the job.

▶ Various types of interviews can occur, including one-on-one interviews, phone interviews, online interviews, and group interviews. Applicants need to be prepared for any interview type they encounter.

▶ Hiring managers expect candidates to come prepared to ask specific questions about the position and the company that are not answered during the interview.

CHECK YOUR UNDERSTANDING

Visit www.cengagebrain.com to see how well you have mastered the material in Chapter 7.

SUGGESTED ITEMS FOR LEARNING PORTFOLIO

▌ Researching Companies: This activity will increase your awareness of important issues at companies of interest and contribute to effective interview skills.

▌ Writing Interview Questions and Answers: Writing interview questions and answers will prepare you to answer actual interview questions more effectively.

▌ Mock Interviews: Practicing interviewing skills in mock interviews will give you practice for an authentic interview.

REFERENCES

Bellevue University Career Services. (n.d.). Strategies for effective interviewing. Retrieved May 14, 2013, from http://www.bellevue.edu/services/content/pdfs/strategies-for-effective-interviewing.pdf

Best-job-interview.com. (2013). Interview body language that sends the right message. Retrieved May 14, 2013, from http://www.best-job-interview.com/interview-body-language.html

Bowman, C. B. (n.d.). Keeping a lid on interview anxiety. Retrieved May 14, 2013, from the Dow Jones Career Journal Europe web site: http://www.careerjournaleurope.com/jobhunting/interviewing/19980812-bowman.html

Careerbuilder.com. (2011). Candidates' most unusual interview mistakes. Retrieved May 14, 2013, from http://thehiringsite.careerbuilder.com/2011/01/12/candidates-most-unusual-interview-mistakes/

Caroselli, M. (n.d.). How to survive a team interview. Retrieved May 16, 2013, from http://www.careerjournaleurope.com/jobhunting/interviewing/19990630-caroselli.html

Dress for Success. (n.d.). Don't leave anything to chance. Remember: you can't be too prepared! Retrieved May 14, 2013, from http://www.dressforsuccess.org/careers_careertips.aspx

Hansen, R. S. (n.d.[a]). The Career Doctor's Cures & Remedies: "What are the most common job-interview questions?" Quintessential Careers. Retrieved May 16, 2013, from http://www.quintcareers.com/career_doctor_cures/job_interview_questions.html

7

Hansen, R. S. (n.d.[b]). Job interviewing do's and don'ts for job seekers. Quintessential Careers. Retrieved May 14, 2013, from http://www.quintcareers.com/interviewing-dos-donts.html

Hansen, R. S. (n.d.[e]). Situational interviews and stress interviews: what to make of them and how to succeed in them. Quintessential Careers. Retrieved May 16, 2013, from http://www.quintcareers.com/situational_stress_interviews.html

Hansen, R. S. (n.d.[c]). Step-by-step guide to researching companies: how to conduct job-search research. Quintessential Careers. Retrieved May 14, 2013, from http://www.quintcareers.com/researching_companies_guide.html

Hansen, R.S. (n.d.[d]). Types of job interviews for job-seekers. Quintessential Careers. Retrieved May 16, 2013, from http://www.quintcareers.com/job_interviews.html

Lewis, K. (2012). The dos and don'ts for addressing weaknesses during an interview. Retrieved May 28, 2013, from http://comerecommended.com/2012/01/the-dos-and-donts-for-addressing-weaknesses-in-an-interview/

Office of Human Resources Management, University of Albany. (n.d.) Retrieved May 16, 2013, from http://www.albany.edu/diversityandinclusion/files/Appendix_14.pdf_legal_andillegal_questions.pdf

Quintessential Careers. (n.d.[a]). Free sample behavioral interview questions for job-seekers. Retrieved May 16, 2013, from http://www.quintcareers.com/sample_behavioral.html

Quintessential Careers. (n.d.[b]). Job-seeker interview database: 20 situational job interview practice questions. Retrieved May 16, 2013, from http://www.quintcareers.com/interview_question_database/situational.html

Quintessential Careers. (n.d.[c]). Questions you can ask at the job interview. Retrieved May 17, 2013, from http://www.quintcareers.com/asking_interview_questions.html

San Francisco State University Student Involvement & Career Center. (n.d.). Tactful answers to illegal interview questions. Retrieved May 16, 2013, from http://www.sfsu.edu/~career/handouts/interviewing/Illegal_Questions.pdf

Santa Clara University Career Center. (n.d.). Interviewing & dressing for success. Retrieved May 14, 2013, from http://www.scu.edu/careercenter/students/prepare/interviewprep/upload/Interviewing-Dressing-2.pdf

Turner, J. (n.d.) Behavioral interviews: a great showcase for you, but you must prepare now. Retrieved May 16, 2013, from http://www.quintcareers.com/behavioral_interview_preparation.html

7

CHAPTER OUTLINE

Ariel Skelley/Getty Images

8

After the Interview

LEARNING OBJECTIVES

By the end of this chapter, you will achieve the following objectives:

▶ Discuss the purpose and methods of follow-up to an interview.

▶ Describe the importance of sending a thank-you note to your interviewer.

▶ List areas that should be evaluated when assessing a job offer.

▶ List some of the more common benefits offered by employers.

▶ Explain the purpose of negotiating.

▶ Discuss how personal, professional, and family goals can influence job negotiations.

▶ Describe the process involved in assessing a job offer.

▶ Understand the benefits typically covered in an employment relocation package.

▶ Explain the steps involved in successful negotiating.

▶ Demonstrate how to effectively negotiate a salary.

▶ Demonstrate the ability to write a letter for declining a job offer.

▶ Describe attitudes that contribute to outcomes of job interviews.

▶ Describe constructive attitudes toward job rejection.

▶ Explain the purpose of getting feedback from the employer when denied a job.

▶ Describe methods of obtaining feedback from employers.

BE IN THE KNOW

What Went Wrong?

So you didn't get the job. The interview went well, you thought, so why didn't you get hired?

The following are some tips to help you evaluate what might have gone wrong during the job search process and some suggestions for improving your ability to land that job.

- **Assess your resumé.** Evaluate your resumé for spelling and grammatical errors. Ensure that it is concise, yet contains detailed, relevant information. Make sure that your resumé clearly summarizes your accomplishments and their results.

- **Examine your goals.** Review your goals and ensure that they are realistic for your level of training and experience. Consider that you may need to take a lower-level position to start. Be sure to also assess how well you are articulating how your skills apply to the needs of the employer. Consider your transferable skills. Are you demonstrating how transferable skills apply to the position? Evaluate your goals to make sure that your skills support them.

- **Get firsthand feedback.** In addition to seeking the feedback of interviewers and contacts at the jobsite, obtain input from a trusted source in your field, such as a friend or colleague, former instructor, or an internship supervisor. The individual should be someone whom you trust, who can be honest with you.

- **Assess your self-presentation.** Your self-presentation includes all of your personal attributes perceived by a potential employer. Your appearance, the attitude that you project, your verbal and nonverbal communication, your ability to respond professionally and effectively to questions, and your general politeness and courtesy all contribute to how you present yourself to interviewers.

- **Reevaluate your job-hunting methods.** Remember the importance of networking and getting your name and credentials in front of potential employers. Review and strengthen your personal brand. Exude professionalism at all times (adapted from Cardillo 2007).

INTERVIEW FOLLOW-UP

Following up after the interview is essential and can be done in a variety of ways. Forbes.com (2012) suggests four ways to follow up after an interview that will not be deemed annoying by the hiring manager.

 Ask about what happens next in the hiring process. At the end of the interview, it is important to ask the employer when further contact from the company should be expected. If you have not received word within the designated timeframe, it is acceptable to contact the employer to ask about the status of the hiring process. If it is necessary to leave a message, provide your correct phone number(s) and the best time to reach

8

you. If you have not received a return call within 24 hours, follow up with another call. Unfortunately, some employers are not considerate in following up with job applicants. If you have had no return calls after leaving two or three messages in a week's time, then it may be necessary to assume that the job has been filled. It may be helpful to contact an individual other than the interviewer at the company, such as the director of human resources, to determine the status of the position. Make sure throughout the process that your efforts do not become bothersome to individuals at the company. Maintain a positive professional demeanor at all times.

▶ **Send a thank-you note.** This should go without saying. The process for sending thank-you notes is discussed in greater detail in the next section.

▶ **Request permission to connect with the hiring manager via LinkedIn.** Do not make this request simply for the sake of asking. Try to create a logical reason for wanting to link to the person during the interview and then make the request at that time. Even if you don't get the job, it is still a valuable way to keep your name in front of the hiring manager should additional opportunities at the company become available. In addition, you may be able to connect with others that can help you in the job search process.

▶ **Do a periodic check-in.** Make checking in with the hiring manager of value. You do not want to ask "did I get the job?" or "has a decision been made about the position?" Instead, use the check-in approach as another networking strategy. Send an article of interest with a short note, for example, but do not ask for, nor expect a response. If you do get one, even if you did not land the job, all the better for you. That means that the hiring manager remembers you and likely appreciates your effort, and who knows where that may lead.

Chris Ryan/OJO Images/Getty Images

Following up an interview with professional behaviors, such as sending a thank-you note, is nearly as important as the interview itself.

THANK-YOU NOTES

There is no more important follow-up to an interview than sending a thank-you note to the interviewer(s). And yet the percentage of interviewees who complete this simple task is staggeringly low (some reports claim less than 50 percent).

8

Sending a thank-you note in a professional setting is not the same as thanking your Aunt Clara for the socks she sent for your tenth birthday. Treat thank-you notes as another form of networking. Not only are you showing good manners by sending a note, you are creating an opportunity to sell your value and reiterate your personal brand to the hiring manager at the same time. Some hiring managers say that if they do not receive an acknowledgment from the candidate, they will no longer be considered for the position. Others say that receiving such correspondence has tipped the hiring scale in favor of that candidate. Do not take chances, send a note!

HANDWRITTEN

The two most common forms of thank-you notes are handwritten and electronic. Thank-you letters can be handwritten only if your handwriting is neat. If not, type the letter and personally sign it. Ensure that the spelling of names and titles is correct. Send your thank-you note as soon as the interview is over. The employer will appreciate your quick response. When sending the note consider including your networking business card, even if you gave the hiring manager one at the time of the interview. This is another opportunity to show your professionalism. Figure 8-1 provides an example of a thank-you letter.

ELECTRONIC

Today, sending an e-mail thank-you note is generally considered very acceptable, although some recruiters and hiring managers might argue otherwise. If you feel that the company's culture is attuned to accepting this form of thank you, then consider going this route. This is also a smart way to go if you know the hiring decision will be made quickly. Even if you sent an e-mail thank you, it is best to follow it up with a written message.

8

CASE IN POINT: DECISIONS, DECISIONS

Read the scenario below. Then, in groups or as a class, answers the questions at the end.

Joe Ward, a recent graduate of his local community college, has been searching for a job. During his job search, he has had numerous interviews with a variety of companies. There are two companies from which Joe would particularly like to receive an offer. If he gets offers from both, Joe is unsure about how he will decide which job to take, because both jobs offer different but excellent opportunities.

Today, Joe received offers for both of the jobs he wanted. One job offers slightly more money than the other but lacks some benefits that the other job offer provides. Joe is faced with a difficult decision.

▶ What should Joe consider when he is trying to make a decision regarding which job offer to accept?

▶ What resources might Joe use to help him make this difficult decision?

▶ What issues do you think are most important for Joe to consider?

▶ In what areas might Joe consider negotiating with the offering companies? If Joe decides to negotiate, what approach should he take with the companies?

▶ Have you ever been in this position? If so, what did you do? Was your choice the best decision? If not, what have you learned from your own experience?

NEGOTIATION

PURPOSE OF NEGOTIATION

Receiving job offers can be both exciting and daunting due to the variety of decisions that must be made. These decisions include whether the offer should be accepted as is or whether further negotiations are necessary. Negotiation can result in an offer more closely matched to your wishes, which will increase your overall satisfaction with the final package. Ultimately, a job applicant wants to be sure that he or she makes the right decision in accepting or declining a position.

The most important issue that applicants have to consider is the effect that accepting or declining a job offer will have on their own personal goals, professional goals, and family goals (Hoover, 2007). It is important to evaluate each of these areas in order to determine

SELF-ASSESSMENT QUESTIONS

- What personal, professional, and family goals do you have that could be affected by the type of job you accept?
- What concerns or fears might you have when it comes to negotiating a job offer?

? CRITICAL THINKING QUESTION

- What is your response to the following statement? "Negotiating skills are overrated. It is totally up to the employer what the job offer will be."

whether negotiations are needed to better satisfy these important goals. For example, the job that you accept can affect your earning potential, which influences your family's goals. Likewise, the setting in which you work will offer you specific opportunities for your professional growth. Being aware of these considerations and needs is essential to effective long-term planning. If you have done effective research (see Chapters 1 and 7) into the companies you are considering, you will have a clear idea of what each offers.

ASSESSING THE ORGANIZATION

Before beginning the application and interviewing process with an organization, an applicant has typically conducted some research to gain knowledge about the organization. Further questions can then be asked of the employer during the interviewing process. Information helpful to research includes areas such as the financial condition of the company and its size, years in existence, and reputation. Knowing these aspects of a company will help you to decide whether the company is a match for your personal and professional goals. This type of information can be accessed using a variety of methods, including conducting research online, where materials such as annual reports, press releases, newspaper articles, and industry publications may be accessed (U.S. Department of Labor, Bureau of Labor Statistics, 2011). Other directories that may be helpful to reference include the following sources, which you may have accessed for preliminary company research:

- *Dun & Bradstreet's Million Dollar Directory*
- *Standard and Poor's Register of Corporations*
- *Mergent's Industrial Review* (formerly *Moody's Industrial Manual*)
- *Thomas Register of American Manufacturers*
- *Ward's Business Directory*

The College at Brockport State University of New York (n.d.) suggests keeping the following questions in mind when evaluating an organization:

1. Does the organization's business or activity match your own interests and beliefs? For example, if you are a healthcare worker but believe abortion is wrong, then working at a facility that performs abortions would not be advised. You

will be more dedicated to an organization that conducts business that matches your interests and beliefs.

2. Will the size of the organization affect you? What is your working environment preference: large firm or small firm? It is important to weigh the pros and cons of what large firms may offer versus smaller firms, including advancement opportunities and breadth and depth of the benefits package.

3. Are you willing to work for a company that is new or does the stability of a well-established organization appeal to you? Some individuals are willing to take the risk with a newer company due to the possibility of sharing in the company's future successes. Others may determine that the possibility of job loss is too high a risk.

4. Does the company offer goods and/or services that appeal to your personal values? Consider if you want to be associated with what the company produces and its corporate reputation and philosophy based upon those products or services.

Understanding the Job

Prior to accepting an offer, it is important for the job applicant to have a clear picture regarding the nature of the job. Areas to consider include those listed here (Brockport State University of New York, n.d.):

▶ Job location

▶ Duties, responsibilities, and hours of the job

▶ Turnover rate of the job—if high, what are the reasons?

▶ Future opportunities available within the organization and how these opportunities can be acquired by accepting the current job offer

▶ Salary and benefits, including pay raises, bonus plans, and continuing education

Negotiable Factors

When an offer is made, it is important to determine what areas can be negotiated. The following factors can often be negotiated (Hoover, 2007):

▶ Location of the position

▶ Relocation benefits

- Start date
- When appraisal reviews will be conducted and salary increases received
- Sign-on bonus
- Salary
- Overall benefits package

Job Location and Relocation Benefits

Advancements in technology and computers have significantly increased flexibility in job location. Many jobs can be performed either at home or at a satellite office. If relocation is required, it is important to research the community in which you would be living to ensure that the location is desirable. If a job applicant must relocate, the company may offer a benefits package to help defray relocation costs. Receiving this benefit does sometimes depend on the level of the position. Many organizations do not offer candidates at an entry-level position a reloca-tion benefits package. If a relocation package is offered, the following benefits may be included (Quintessential Careers, n.d.[b]):

- House-hunting trip expenses
- Lodging fees
- Moving expenses
- Mortgage/closing fees
- Brokerage fees
- Temporary housing expenses
- Spouse reemployment expenses

Start Date

Even though the employer may have a specific start date for begin-ning work, this does not mean that negotiating a different start date is impossible. Negotiating a start date is important, depending on the applicant's situation. It is better to inform the employer of any issues that require a postponement of the start date than to accept the start date with full knowledge of conflicts that may create problems later.

Schedules of Appraisal Reviews and Salary Increases

Some employers give bonuses for job performance. Salary increases are often attached to appraisal reviews. "If the organization incorporates

8

this type of appraisal system, it might be possible to ask for an earlier review to increase your earnings sooner than normal" (Hoover, 2007, "Factors That May Be Negotiated").

Sign-On Bonuses

Sign-on bonuses may be an option, depending on the industry you are entering. A sign-on bonus is "an agreed upon amount of money given to you at the time of your acceptance of the offer" (Hoover, 2007, "Factors That May Be Negotiated"). If the employer's need for your expertise is high, it may be possible to negotiate a larger sign-on bonus.

Salary

Prior to applying for any position, job applicants need to determine the potential salary range for each job and how that compares to their budget requirements. Applying for a job that offers a salary significantly lower than your budget requirements is not wise. If the expected salary is close to the required amount, then it may be realistic to negotiate the desired salary. Job applicants should always establish a minimum salary requirement. It is also important to understand the difference between hiring range and salary range. Hiring range is the range within which a starting salary is determined, based on the expertise of the new hire. Salary range is the range of the salary for the position over the course of employment. The top of the salary range indicates the highest amount you can earn in that position unless the range is increased. Hiring range is where you will start on the pay scale. Salary range has more long-lasting implications, as it tells you the maximum amount you can expect to earn over time in the position. Knowing your personal and professional goals will help you to determine whether the salary range is appropriate for you.

Your minimum salary requirement is based on your financial needs. By setting a realistic budget, job applicants can more clearly differentiate needs from desires. Finding a high-paying entry-level job may not be realistic. Establishing what is realistic will assist you in making wise choices.

Another determining factor affecting salary is the reality of what can be earned for the type of position and industry you are entering. It is reasonable to want to earn as high a salary as possible, but it is irrational and frustrating to expect an unrealistic amount. It is wise to research a realistic salary so that your expectations are realistic. Consider the following resources for researching salaries:

▶ Salary.com

▶ Payscale.com

▶ JobStar: Profession-Specific Salary Surveys

▶ SalaryExpert.com

▶ Bureau of Labor Statistics

▶ Securities and Exchange Commission

▶ The American Almanac of Jobs and Salaries

▶ Professional trade journals and business magazines

▶ Newspaper and online job listings

Establishing the acceptable range allows for the job applicant to more accurately access what the employer is willing to do. If hiring and salary ranges are below your expectations, begin the negotiation process, which will be discussed in the subsequent sections of this chapter.

Typically, a salary offer is not made until all interviews have been completed. An offer can be written or verbal. If an offer comes in person or by phone, you need not accept the offer at that very moment. It is always good to ask for some time to consider all the details of the job offer, including the salary. The following are some other tips for negotiating salary (Hansen, n.d; CollegeGrad.com, n.d.):

▶ **Know the reasonable limits.** Complete effective industry research to determine the realistic salary range in your field. Know what is fair considering your geographic region, education, and demand for employees in your industry. You don't want to undersell yourself, nor do you want to price yourself out of the running.

▶ **Aim high.** When negotiating a salary, it is wise to request (within reason) a higher salary than what you are willing to accept. The employer is likely to make a lower counterproposal to your offer, so by proposing a higher amount, you are more likely to complete your negotiations closer to your goal. A key factor in the success of this approach is to keep your request within reasonable limits.

▶ **Negotiate to your strength.** If you are a skilled speaker, ask to discuss a counterproposal in a meeting. If you communicate better in writing, then send a counterproposal letter. Examples of counterproposal letters can be found on the Internet. Conduct a search using "salary counterproposal letters" as your search terms.

▶ **Avoid (as much as possible) naming a specific salary.** During the interviewing process, the employer may ask you what your salary expectations are. When this occurs, it is wise not to mention a specific amount to avoid losing out by stating too low a salary or, conversely, missing out on the job because you have asked for an unrealistic sum. If you have completed effective industry research, you will know what is fair. If you are asked about your salary requirements, it is wise to respond by asking what the hiring range is for new graduates in the position. Respond by indicating whether the range is acceptable or not. You can tactfully indicate that the range is competitive with or below that offered by other organizations.

▶ **Remember other benefits in the package.** If the salary is not negotiable, consider negotiating other benefits. For example, you may request a signing bonus, higher performance bonuses, or a performance review and raise to be completed sooner than is typical. Examples of nonmonetary benefits to consider include time off, a flexible work schedule, or other benefits such as insurance packages.

▶ **Negotiate with a win-win attitude.** Realize that you need to exhibit flexibility when possible. Hansen (n.d.) suggests, "Never make demands. Instead, raise questions and make requests during negotiations. Keep the tone conversational, not confrontational." Negotiations must be done professionally and thoughtfully if you really want the job.

8

success steps for preparing for negotiating

- Know the reasonable limits.
- Negotiate to your strength. For example, if you communicate most effectively in writing, negotiate in writing.
- Aim high.
- Remember other benefits in the package. These can also be negotiated.
- Negotiate with a win–win attitude.

apply it

Salary Research

GOAL: *To develop an awareness of a realistic salary expectation in a specific field*

STEP 1: Conduct research on the Internet and/or at the library regarding the salary ranges you are likely to find in your field.

STEP 2: Write a brief report summarizing your findings.

STEP 3: Consider placing the salary research in your Learning Portfolio.

8

Keith Brofsky/Getty Images

Developing your negotiating skills as well as gaining as much knowledge as possible about a company will support your efforts to achieve your employment goals.

Overall Benefits Package

Although salary is a critical aspect of a job, the benefits package can often compensate for a less desirable salary. It is important for job applicants to understand and appreciate that benefits can add up to 30% of the total compensation package (Quintessential Careers, n.d.[a]). Following are some of the more common benefits offered by employers:

- Medical insurance
- Dental insurance
- Optical/eye care insurance
- Life insurance
- Accidental death insurance
- Business travel insurance
- Disability insurance

- Vacation days
- Paid holidays
- Sick/personal days/family leave
- 401(k) plan
- Pension plan
- Profit sharing
- Stock options/Employee Stock Ownership Plan (ESOP)
- Tuition reimbursement
- Health club membership
- Parking, commuting, and business expense reimbursement

DOs AND DON'Ts IN NEGOTIATING

Because the ultimate goal of negotiating is to get what you want, developing effective negotiating skills is critical to success. Kelly (2001) presents the following steps to successful negotiating:

- **Step 1: Prepare.** Knowing a company's hiring practices and goals will inform you of the company's priorities and define the value of the skills that you bring to the organization's long-term plans. Use the research you have completed to prepare yourself with this critical knowledge.

- **Step 2: Know what you can about the hiring dynamics.** If you are a highly desirable candidate because of your expertise or because you are one of a few or the only applicant, your strategies will be different than if you were one of several qualified applicants. Knowing the dynamics of the hiring situation will define the amount of bargaining leverage that you have.

- **Step 3: Be professional.** The individuals with whom you are negotiating are your potential coworkers. Negotiate in a manner that demonstrates your professionalism.

- **Step 4: Know your needs and limits.** Entering the negotiation process with a clear understanding of your own needs will allow you to negotiate reasonably. A clear picture of what you need and want as well as issues on which you can yield will allow you to more easily see whether and when negotiations have succeeded or failed.

- **Step 5: Respect the employer's position.** As you have limits regarding what you can and cannot accept, so does the employer. Be aware and respectful of budget constraints and other limitations, such as fairness to current employees of the employer. You are not expected to accept something that cannot meet your needs, but it is important to recognize when the employer cannot go beyond certain limitations.

▶ **Step 6: Use your judgment.** Remember that what you say during the negotiation process is up to you. Of course, be honest, but approach problems and concerns in a manner that helps your position. Total candor is not always necessary and may not be appropriate in all situations. By divulging too much, you may be offered less than what the company was willing to offer you originally.

▶ **Step 7: Remember that there's more than salary.** Remember that you have other points of negotiation in addition to salary. If it fits your needs, you can also negotiate for an earlier performance review and raise, request additional time off in lieu of pay, or bargain for other available benefits.

▶ **Step 8: Stay focused on your goal.** Your goal in the negotiation process is to achieve an employment package that meets your needs. The negotiation process is not one of winning or losing, but one of reaching a mutually agreeable employment situation. Don't focus on winning, and never make the employer feel as if he or she were a loser.

▶ **Step 9: Remain objective.** Part of professionalism is remaining objective and rational. State your position clearly and without signs of emotion. Emotional outbursts diminish your professionalism and are likely to work against you in the negotiation process.

▶ **Step 10: Know when to stop.** Know when you have achieved your goal or when it is clear that the employer is unable to meet your requests. Likewise, do not push for more than you reasonably need. Avoid appearing greedy and unreasonable, which may cause the employer to reconsider the offer that has been made.

▶ **Step 11: Get it in writing.** As with any business transaction, it is important to get a written agreement summarizing the offer. If possible, have an attorney review the written agreement to ensure that all elements are appropriately documented prior to accepting the offer.

Self-Assessment Questions

- What areas of negotiation do you know you need to work on?
- How do you plan on improving your negotiation skills?

? Critical Thinking Question

▶ What is your response to the following statement? "Men are better at negotiating than women."

8

success steps for negotiating salary successfully

- Prepare.
- Know what you can about the hiring dynamics.
- Be professional.
- Know your needs and limits.
- Respect the employer's position.
- Use your judgment.
- Remember that there's more than salary.
- Remain goal directed.
- Remain objective.
- Know when to stop.
- Get it in writing.

Effective negotiation can lead to an employment agreement that is acceptable to both employer and applicant. In addition, it is wise to obtain a copy of the agreement in writing.

apply it

Negotiating a Salary

GOAL: To demonstrate the ability to effectively negotiate a salary

STEP 1: Divide students in the class into pairs.

STEP 2: Using scenarios provided by the instructor, role-play negotiating a salary with an employer. One student will be the employer and the other student the job applicant. Treat the role-playing seriously, because this activity can help prepare you for real-life salary negotiation situations. After the role-playing is completed, the "employer" should constructively critique the job applicant on his or her negotiation abilities. Where could the job applicant improve? What did the applicant do right? If needed, redo the role-playing to provide practice in negotiation skills. Reverse roles to allow for each student to represent the employer and the job applicant.

STEP 3: Write a brief report on what you learned from this activity and consider putting this information in your Learning Portfolio.

ACCEPTING OR DECLINING A JOB OFFER

When accepting a job offer, it is important to make sure that what is agreed upon is documented in writing. This documentation typically comes from the company in the form of a letter of offer or letter of agreement. If this is not a common practice of the employer, ask the employer to provide you a letter of agreement that briefly outlines what has been discussed. Inform the employer that you need to have some sort of documentation of agreement for your own personal records. This should not be an issue and later may protect you if any disagreements occur. Make sure to obtain this documentation prior to your start date.

If you verbally decline an offer, it is still important to write a professional letter declining the offer (Machowski, n.d.). Always respond to an employer's offer. Not responding is unprofessional and takes up valuable time that the employer will need to find another applicant.

When preparing the letter of decline, keep in mind the following four steps suggested by Machowski (n.d.):

▶ **Step 1.** Call the employer to decline the offer and then send a formal letter to decline the offer. Send the letter immediately after the employer has been verbally informed.

▶ **Step 2.** Prepare the letter as you would any other professional correspondence. Respond professionally and courteously so that you maintain a professional relationship with the organization. The contacts at this company may be worth having in the future.

▶ **Step 3.** In the letter, there is no need to discuss in detail your future plans or why you are declining. It is acceptable to say that you have decided on a different position that more closely matches your career objectives. Be gracious and express your appreciation for the offer. State your positive impression

SELF-ASSESSMENT QUESTION

- What has your experience been so far regarding accepting or declining an offer from an employer? Did you at any time feel as if you could have handled the situation more professionally? If so, how will you improve your methods next time?

apply it

Letter to Decline a Job Offer

GOAL: To demonstrate the ability to write a letter declining a job offer

STEP 1: Conduct research on the Internet and/or library to find examples of letters for declining job offers.

STEP 2: Create your own letter utilizing the examples as a guide. The letter should be representative of what you would send to an employer. Give your first draft to your instructor for review. Write a final draft incorporating your instructor's feedback and representing what would be sent to the employer.

STEP 3: Consider placing the examples and your Letter to Decline a Job Offer in your Learning Portfolio.

8

of the company and let the company know that you seriously considered the offer.

▶ **Step 4.** Be clear and concise. Say what needs to be said and then end the letter professionally.

Sample letters for declining a job offer can be found on the Internet. Conduct a search using "letters for declining a job" as your search term.

 ## DEALING WITH REJECTION

Although it is likely that no one enjoys rejection of any kind, being declined for a job or being denied an interview *is* a part of the job search process. Receiving a rejection letter can be a positive way to develop your skills and expand your opportunities. Having the proper mindset and using rejection as a way to learn about yourself and develop weak areas are significant aspects of approaching rejection with a positive attitude.

BEING DECLINED IS PART OF THE JOB SEARCH

Gordon (2003) reminds us that elimination from consideration for a position is a normal part of the job search. She emphasizes that the way you view not being hired is instrumental in continuing the job search with a positive attitude. Accepting that a certain amount of rejection is to be expected in your search will prepare you for the inevitable. You may feel disappointment, but you will be more likely to see being turned away from a job in its proper perspective.

SELF-REFLECTION IS CRITICAL

Having the ability to look at yourself and evaluate your strengths and weaknesses is an essential element of using rejection as a positive experience. Self-assessment will help you to look objectively at yourself and set appropriate goals for your development according to the demands of your field. You can use rejection as a vehicle for accomplishing this and moving closer to achieving your professional goals. Record your self-reflection and observations in a journal to review your responses as you conduct your search.

8

apply it

Job Search Journal

GOAL: *To develop insight into your perspectives on the job search, maintain a positive mindset, and track the outcomes of your search*

STEP 1: Create a journal (hard copy or electronic) that you will use on a consistent basis throughout your job search. Select a format that is convenient and appealing to you and that you will use.

STEP 2: Record the events of your job search. Include both positive and disappointing incidents as well as your emotional reactions to each. Examine each reaction and make a judgment regarding whether it is a constructive response.

STEP 3: If your response is less than constructive, apply one of the techniques discussed in this chapter. Look for the opportunities that present themselves throughout your search and take note of them. Record your responses to the process, including changes in your perspective.

STEP 4: Note the actions that you choose to take based on your changed perspective. Compare these actions to those that you might have taken if you had a less positive mindset.

STEP 5: Note the outcomes of your positive actions.

STEP 6: Consider placing your journal entries in your Learning Portfolio.

AN ATTITUDE FOR SUCCESS

In addition to developing effective interviewing skills and job search strategies, there are actions you can take to prepare yourself for rejection when it occurs. Remember that being declined for a percentage of positions or not being called for an interview is inevitable. Assuming the appropriate outlook on the job application process can put you in a healthier frame of mind. The following suggestions for preparing your perspective on possible rejection are adapted from Bellm (2007):

▶ **Tell yourself it's not personal.** It's not nice getting rejected and it's easy to take that rejection personally. Dismiss the emotional attachment from the rejection and move forward.

▶ **Keep a log or journal of your successes.** Write down all the positives that have happened during your job search, whether it's an interview that went well or a compliment on your portfolio. Revisit these success stories to remind yourself that you have many strengths going for you.

8

▶ **Tell yourself that you are worthy.** This is a personal value that you must hold onto. It is not your lot in life to have only bad things happen to you.

▶ **Get a lot of things going at once.** If you only have one resumé out there and you get a rejection letter, you are starting from scratch each time. Have several resumés out in the field at the same time. Continue and strengthen your networking strategies. There will be some positive results that will help offset the negative ones.

▶ **Remember, it's a numbers game.** The odds are just not very good of landing your ideal position right out of the chute. Understand that you will most likely have a set of failures before success in your job search. Look past the bad parts and into the good parts.

▶ **Avoid the negative.** When you are anticipating something, it is often easy to become anxious and recall bad experiences or failures. Doing so may cause you to anticipate negative outcomes and behave in a manner that invites disappointment. Be careful not to anticipate negative outcomes that can exaggerate your fears. Sanford (2009) states that even though unemployment is at 9 percent, 91 percent of the workforce is employed. Regardless of the economic climate, companies continue to hire. "People leave their jobs willingly every day to change roles, retire, move, raise families, return to school, start their own ventures, or volunteer. Each one of these circumstances leaves an opening and is far more common than a business adding to staff due to a growth spurt or new product launch," says Sanford.

SELF-ASSESSMENT QUESTIONS

- How do you typically respond to rejection or disappointment?
- Do you believe your response is negative or positive?
- How would you change your response?

? CRITICAL THINKING QUESTIONS

▶ What steps can you take to make your responses to rejection or disappointment more positive?
▶ How would doing so contribute to your success in the job search process?

---

success steps for attitudes for success

- Tell yourself it's not personal.
- Keep a log or journal of your successes.
- Tell yourself that you are worthy.
- Get a lot of applications going at once.
- Remember, it's a numbers game.
- Avoid the negative.

8

KEEPING A PERSPECTIVE ON REJECTION

Putting yourself in a healthy frame of mind can lessen the blow of learning you were not hired, but positive thinking will not entirely eliminate its occurrence. The manner in which you view a situation has significant impact on the way you feel about it, think about it, and respond. When you are declined for a position, carefully assess how you are thinking about the situation. Keep the following points in mind:

▶ **Rejection is not a reflection of your skills or worth.** Companies have numerous criteria for hiring, including specific needs, timing, and other factors of which you might not be aware. Reasons for your not being hired can be many and varied, none of which reflect on your professional talent (Gordon, 2003).

▶ **Being declined is a small piece of the bigger picture.** Gordon (2003) points out that the emotional impact of rejection is a short-term price to pay for the longer-term satisfaction of a rewarding career. Focus on the characteristics you are developing that will be valuable to you in the long term, such as self-confidence and the ability to communicate with many types of professionals.

▶ **There might be something better out there.** Dattani (n.d.) points out that rejections sometimes pave the way for greater success. Dattani gives the example of J. K. Rowling, author of the famed *Harry Potter* books, who was initially turned down by several publishers in Britain before her now-famous books were accepted for publication. Another example that Dattani cites is film director Steven Spielberg, who was refused admission to the University of Southern California because of a low grade-point average. If you don't get your first choice now, know that there might be something better waiting for you.

▶ **Look for opportunities and what you can learn.** As with many adverse situations, opportunity can grow from rejection. There is much to be learned from rejection, including insights about your presentation, skills you need to develop, and improved interviewing skills.

8

CRITICAL THINKING QUESTION

▶ What other methods can you think of that would contribute to maintaining a positive perspective?

> **success steps for keeping a perspective on rejection**
>
> - Rejection is not a reflection of your skills or worth.
> - Being declined is a small piece of the bigger picture.
> - There might be something better out there.
> - Look for opportunities and what you can learn.

GETTING FEEDBACK

Once you have adopted a healthy perspective on being declined for a job or not getting an interview, you are ready to make the best of the situation by learning as much as you can from the experience. Opportunities include gaining insight into your interviewing proficiency, learning where your technical skills can be improved, and increasing your chances for expanded networking. Consider the following possibilities for learning from rejection:

▶ **Apply what you have learned.** There is much to be learned in the job-seeking and interviewing process. Being required to interact with other professionals, market your expertise, and use effective communication are just some of the skills you will practice during the job search. Paying attention to the effectiveness of these skills can provide insight into how you can polish and develop your professional presentation. Even if you are denied a position, use the experience to evaluate and improve your skills.

▶ **Follow up with the interviewer or contact person.** Measom (n.d.) suggests that most rejected candidates do not make the effort to write a thank-you note to the person(s) who sent the rejection letter. Reasons for sending a brief yet sincere note include the following:

- It makes a positive statement.
- Thanking the interviewer for his or her time and consideration of your qualifications may lead to some additional contacts.

8

▶ Job-Employment-Guide (2009) suggests that the follow-up letter contain the following elements:

- Appreciation for letting you know the results, even though you are disappointed at not getting the position

- Appreciation for the time, effort, and thoughtfulness given to you by interviewers

- Appreciation for the opportunity to get to know the organization and its people, and what impressed you about it

- A statement of your continued interest in the organization

- A request to contact you if another suitable position becomes available or if the status of the current position changes

▶ **Use rejection as an opportunity to learn.** Being declined for a position can be a valuable learning experience. It is appropriate and effective to contact the interviewer and request feedback regarding why you were not considered for the position. Express appreciation for the interviewer's assistance during the interview process, as well as your disappointment in not being selected. Explain that you are interested in developing and improving your skills, and feedback would be helpful. Specifically, ask for feedback on skills that you might develop, ways that you might improve your resumé, and other information that would be helpful to you in your situation. Respond to any feedback professionally and with an open mind. Thank the individual for his or her time, honesty, and assistance.

▶ **Apply feedback to your professional development.** Use the feedback that you receive to assess your skills, improve the quality of your resumé, and enhance your job search strategies. Seriously and thoughtfully consider how you might incorporate the feedback into your professional plan. Set goals and identify strategies for meeting them. For example, if you receive feedback that you seemed to lack knowledge about certain aspects of your field, determine what you need to learn, identify resources for doing so, and set a plan in place for completing your goal by a specific date.

SELF-ASSESSMENT QUESTIONS

- Have you ever turned a disappointment into an opportunity?
- Recall the circumstances. What did you think about in order to see the opportunity? What action did you take?

8

? CRITICAL THINKING QUESTION

▶ What other techniques might you use to turn disappointment into an opportunity?

success steps for creating opportunity from rejection

- Apply what you have learned.
- Follow up with the interviewer or contact person.
- Use rejection as an opportunity to learn.
- Apply feedback to your professional development.

apply it

Asking for Feedback

GOAL: To increase your comfort and skills in requesting feedback after being declined for a position

STEP 1: Form small groups of four students each. Two students will be the interviewers and two, the job applicants.

STEP 2: Allow several minutes for the interviewers to write a script for giving feedback to the job applicants and for the applicants to prepare to ask for feedback. Note that it may be more difficult for the applicants to prepare because, as it would be in reality, they will not know what feedback they are going to receive. Applicants should prepare in a general way.

STEP 3: Role-play the scenarios that you have created. The pair of students not role-playing should observe and provide feedback following the role-plays.

STEP 4: Change roles and repeat the process.

STEP 5: Determine how you will incorporate the feedback that you receive into your interviewing and job search activities.

STEP 6: Consider placing your script and notes of the feedback that you receive in your Learning Portfolio.

8

An effective follow-up letter after being declined for a job will express appreciation for the interviewer's time, state positive impressions of the organization, and reiterate your interest in the company.

Your Name
Your Address
City, State, Zip Code
Date

Interviewer's Name
Name of Organization
Address
City, State, Zip Code

Dear Mr. or Ms. _____:

Thank you for your follow-up letter regarding the computer programming position at XYZ Corporation. Although I was disappointed at not being considered for the position, I do appreciate your getting back to me, as well as the time and consideration given to me by the XYZ staff.

I very much enjoyed meeting you and _____ (insert names of other individuals you met during the interview process). I was especially impressed with the new computer systems you are developing, which clearly demonstrates XYZ's commitment to leadership in technology.

I remain interested in contributing my skills to your organization. Please feel free to contact me if a position suited to my qualifications becomes available or if the status of the programming position changes.

Thank you again for your time and assistance.

Sincerely,

Your Name

CHAPTER SUMMARY

This chapter focused on interview follow-up and the elements of job negotiation. You learned appropriate interview follow-up techniques, such as sending thank-you notes to the interviewer(s) and appropriately maintaining contact with the employer to track the outcome of the interview. Additionally, you learned the many areas to consider when negotiating a job, including personal, professional, and family goals. In addition to these areas, aspects of the job, such as the nature of the job, growth potential, and salary and benefits, must be considered. You learned strategies for negotiation as well as methods for accepting and declining offers.

This chapter also explored job rejection as an expected part of the job search. First, self-reflection is essential for understanding your reaction to rejection. Second, mindset was discussed as a critical part of approaching rejection in a positive way. You were encouraged to keep a positive perspective on rejection and to use it as a learning experience. The basis for doing this is to see the possibilities in rejection and to take advantage of opportunity. You learned steps for obtaining feedback from interviewers.

◉ POINTS TO KEEP IN MIND

In this chapter, several main points were discussed in detail:

▶ Follow-up after the interview is essential and can be done in a variety of ways, including sending an e-mail, writing a letter, and making calls. Calls and e-mails should *always* be followed with written correspondence.

▶ When considering a job offer, the most important issue that applicants need to consider is the effect that the decision to accept or decline will have on their personal, professional, and family goals.

▶ Assessing a job offer entails evaluating areas such as the organization, the nature of the job, future opportunities, salary, and benefits.

▶ Areas that are typically negotiable include location of the position, relocation benefits, starting date, when appraisal reviews will be conducted, when salary increases will be received, sign-on bonus, salary, and overall benefits package.

▶ Prior to accepting any job offer, job applicants should ask for some time to consider all the details.

▶ Negotiating successfully requires being prepared.

▶ A good negotiator seeks a win–win situation for everyone.

▶ Prior to accepting a job offer, always get a written statement of employment terms.

▶ Declining a job offer should be done both verbally and in writing.

▶ Recognize that rejection is a normal part of the job search.

▶ It is important to develop strong self-reflection skills so you can learn from the job search and will be able to view rejection as a positive experience.

▶ Preparing your mindset and keeping a perspective on rejection can help keep you in a positive frame of mind.

8

▶ Rejection during the job search can be turned into an opportunity.

CHECK YOUR UNDERSTANDING

 Visit www.cengagebrain.com to see how well you have mastered the material in Chapter 8.

SUGGESTED ITEMS FOR LEARNING PORTFOLIO

▶ Salary Research: This activity will give you an understanding of realistic salary ranges in your field.

▶ Negotiating a Salary: This activity is intended to provide you with practice in developing your negotiation skills.

▶ Letter to Decline a Job Offer: This activity is intended to provide you with practice declining a job. Feedback that you receive will allow you to develop your skills.

▶ Reflection Questions and Answers.

▶ Job Search Journal: This activity is designed to help you develop insight into your job search attitudes and strategies.

▶ Asking for Feedback: The purpose of this activity is to develop your ability to ask for feedback following being declined a position.

REFERENCES

Bellm, D. (2007). Dealing with failure and rejection in a job search. Retrieved May 20, 2013, from http://www.associatedcontent.com /article/133661/dealing_with_failure_and_rejection.html?cat=72

Cardillo, D. (2007). Job-hunting challenges take some troubleshooting. Retrieved May 28, 2013, from http://www.dcardillo.com/articles /job-hunt.html

The College of Brockport State University of New York. (n.d.). Things to consider when evaluating a job. Retrieved May 21, 2013, from http:// www.brockport.edu/career/jobsearch/List_of_things_to_consider _when_evaluating_a_job.pdf

CollegeGrad.com. (n.d.). The money response technique. Retrieved May 20, 2013, from http://www.collegegrad.com/jobsearch/16-29.shtml

8

Dattani, M. (n.d.). Dealing with rejection. ivillage.co.uk. Retrieved May 20, 2013, from http://www.ivillage.co.uk/workcareer/survive /persondev/articles/0,607356_661149,00.html

Forbes.com. (2012). 4 non-annoying ways to follow up after an interview. Retrieved May 20, 2013, from http://www.forbes.com /sites/dailymuse/2012/05/30/4-non-annoying-ways-to-follow-up -after-an-interview/

Gordon, J. (2003). Top 10 ways to deal with job rejection. Retrieved May 20, 2013, from http://www.qualitycoaching.com/Articles/rejection.html

Hansen, R. S. (n.d.). Job offer too low? Use these key salary negotiation techniques to write a counterproposal letter. Quintessential Careers. Retrieved May 20, 2013, from http://www.quintcareers.com/salary _counter_proposal.html

Hoover, Myrna. (2007). Negotiating job offers guide. The Career Center, Florida State University. Retrieved May 20, 2013, from http:// www.career.fsu.edu/employment/negotiating-offers-guide.html

Job-Employment-Guide. (2009). Responding to employment rejection letter. Retrieved May 20, 2013, from http://www.job-employment -guide.com/employment-rejection-letter.html

Kelly, S. (2001). The dos and don'ts of negotiation. Network World. Retrieved May 20, 2013, from the ITworld.com Site Network Web site: http://www.itworld.com/ITW2109

Machowski, D. A. (n.d.). Declining a job offer. Mount Holyoke College Career Development Center. Retrieved May 20, 2013, from http:// www.mtholyoke.edu/cdc/declining.html

Measom, C. (n.d.). How to write thank you letters after rejection. Retrieved May 21, 2013, from http://work.chron.com/write-thank -letters-after-rejection-2866.html

Quintessential Careers. (n.d.[a]). Salary negotiation and job offer tutorial: Evaluate the entire compensation package. Retrieved May 20, 2013, from http://www.quintcareers.com/salary_package.html

Quintessential Careers. (n.d.[b]). Salary negotiation and job offer tutorial: Relocation expenses. Retrieved May 20, 2013, from http://www .quintcareers.com/salary_relocation.html

Sanford, D. (2009). Staying positive during the job search. Retrieved May 20, 2013, from http://www.boston.com/jobs/news/articles /2009/04/24/staying_positive_during_the_job_search/

U.S. Department of Labor, Bureau of Labor Statistics. (2011). Focused job seeking: a measured approach for looking for work. Retrieved May 20, 2013, from http://www.bls.gov/opub/ooq/2011/spring/art01.pdf

8

CHAPTER OUTLINE

© Stephen Coburn/Shutterstock.com

Professionalism in the Workplace

LEARNING OBJECTIVES

By the end of this chapter, you will achieve the following objectives:

▶ Identify how to enter the workforce.

▶ Explain strategies for re-entering the workforce.

▶ Define professionalism as it pertains to the workplace.

▶ Discuss the elements of professionalism that should be demonstrated in the workplace.

▶ Explain the importance of teamwork in the workplace.

▶ Identify ways to balance work life with personal life.

▶ Describe the importance of lifelong learning.

BE IN THE KNOW

Teamwork

You may have heard the expression "There is no *I* in team." While this statement is both literally and figuratively true, there are several "I" statements of which you should be aware as they pertain to being a successful team member in the workplace.

Consider the following points. Read them and put yourself in a team situation. Do you agree with these statements as they apply to you? What actions might you take to make yourself a better team member?

- *I* need to be accountable to my team members to complete the work I have been assigned.
- *I* am as valued as a team member as anyone else in the team.
- *I* value the contributions of all team members.
- *I* fully participate in discussions and decisions that affect the outcome of the project.
- *I* am a team leader and other team members look to me to fill that role.

- *I* weigh all suggestions equally before coming to a conclusion.
- *I* care about the success of the project as much for my team members as I do for myself.
- *I* meet or exceed deadlines and provide quality work that positively affects the outcome of the project.
- *I* voice my opinions and concerns to the team in order to make the project as successful as possible.
- *I* recognize that different team members bring different skills to the team.

What other "I" statements can you think of as they relate to being a successful team member? GO TEAM!

ENTERING THE WORKFORCE

So far in this text you have learned about the many components that make up a winning job search. And you have succeeded in landing that oh-so-important first "professional" job. Congratulations to you! The next step is to enter the workforce. But how do you transition from life as a successful college student to life as a valued employee?

Hansen and Hansen (n.d.) identify several areas of your life that will change once you enter the workforce. These include the following:

▶ **Time may not be on your side.** Semester breaks. Long summer vacations. Time off for the holidays. Only afternoon

9

classes or perhaps only classes three days a week. What does that add up to? A lot of time that you have for yourself. Unless you worked part time or full time while in school, you may not be ready for the reality that is the 40-hour (and perhaps longer) workweek. Being late to work is not an option if you want to stay employed, and extended vacation time is a thing of the past, at least at this point in your career. Time management may also become more of an issue than it was in college as you struggle to balance your work life with your personal life. (Read more about work-life balance later in this chapter.)

▶ **Act your (work) age.** You may be new to the work environment and your company, but you must act in a professional manner at all times. Just as you sought to act professionally during your job search by being on time, being courteous, dressing properly for interviews, and the like, those traits need to carry forward to your place of employment, but at an even greater and more expanded level. (Read more about professionalism later in this chapter.)

▶ **Follow the yellow brick road, or not.** While you are embarking on your first job, it may not mean that will be the industry or career that you will work in forever. Gone are the days of "womb to tomb" employment, where employees start with a company either right out of high school or college and then retire from that same organization many years later. Nowadays, not only is it very likely that you will change jobs (and perhaps even after only one year in your current position), but you may change careers as well. A college education in almost any field will give you an opportunity to succeed in the business world. Given that, aim for jobs that interest you and that will make you satisfied, not jobs that you feel obligated to accept because they are a part of your major. Just remember to carry (and continue to accumulate) those transferable skills with you as you seek better jobs going forward.

▶ **The Boy Scout motto "Be Prepared" likely isn't true.** By definition, you will not know everything about your job when you first start. Hansen and Hansen point to interviews with recent graduates who stated that college life did not sufficiently prepare them for a variety of college-to-career transition issues, including understanding the work-life balance, the

9

importance of dealing with multiple types of people and personalities, and the reliance on teamwork skills in the workplace, to name a few.

Remember back to when you first started your education and the excitement, and wonder, and nervousness you felt at that time? Starting your career will bring back all of those emotions, and more. The secret is to apply what you learned at school, transition those skills and knowledge to the workplace, and continue to learn, learn, learn.

CASE IN POINT: REMEMBER ME?

Read the scenario below. Then, in groups or as a class, answer the questions at the end.

Sondra Willis is a thirty-five-year-old stay-at-home mom with two children, ages 7 and 5. Sondra has a degree in accounting and was gainfully employed until she left her company to start her family. Sondra, for both economic and personal reasons, is ready to re-enter the workforce.

▶ What should Sondra's approach be to starting her job search?

▶ What tools and resources should Sondra use to aid her in her search?

▶ Should Sondra consider a career change in order to become employed?

▶ What sort of timeline should Sondra give herself for finding employment?

▶ What steps can Sondra take to create an effective work-life balance for herself and her family?

RE-ENTERING THE WORKFORCE

People have many reasons for leaving the workforce, including becoming a full-time parent, returning to school to finish a degree, taking time to travel, or for medical reasons, among others. When a person decides to re-enter the job market, sometimes five, seven, or

9

even ten years after their last job, they often find that the job search landscape has changed since they were last employed.

Sharon Abboud, a writer specializing in career and education issues, offers these strategies for job seekers looking to transition back into the workforce.

▶ **Awaken your network.** Most jobs come from some sort of connection you have (or had). To jump-start your network again, join or rejoin and become active in professional organizations. Read industry journals and get up to speed on new technology and other trends within your industry. Ignite your professional social networking by joining LinkedIn and other sites. Get the word out and let everyone know, including your professional and personal contacts, that you are actively looking to return to the job market. Informational interviews can also reacquaint you with your industry and the types of jobs that might now be available that weren't when you were working.

▶ **Do a resumé makeover.** Evaluate your resumé. It will need updating if it contains any of the following:

  • **Outdated industry technology skills.** Read current job descriptions within your field to discern what employers are looking for today. Determine which skills you are missing and devise a plan to fill those gaps. Attending adult education classes, college classes, or online classes are good solutions.

  • **Use current industry terminology.** Every industry changes, and so does the terminology that describes it. Read trade journals or other professional publications to glean what terms are being used today and what they mean.

  • **Research how resumés are prepared and presented today.** The chances are very good that the resumé you have from even a couple of years ago does not reflect the current trends in resumé writing. There are myriad online sources that provide examples of different resumé types. Study them and decide which approach is best for your field (Walker, n.d.).

▶ **Consider a career change.** Having been out of the job market for a period of time, is this an opportunity to shift gears and start a new career? As you learned, many people do change careers during their work life, so perhaps now is the time to try something new that you've wanted to pursue.

9

SELF-ASSESSMENT QUESTION

- What other changes to your resumé might be needed in order to bring it current?

? CRITICAL THINKING QUESTION

▶ What additional steps can you take to broaden your professional network?

Re-entering the workforce may provide you with an opportunity to make the career change you have always wanted to make.

▶ **Contact your former employer.** It may be a long shot, but if you were well liked in your previous position and were considered a good performer, your employer may still value you. With workplace protocol changing, perhaps there is an opportunity to telecommute, work part time, or come back on board as a consultant.

▶ **Contemplate the work-life balancing act.** Your life's priorities outside of work may not give you the time to devote to a job the way you did before. Seek to balance what you want from life with what your employer wants from you.

▶ **Expect that finding a job will not happen overnight.** Be realistic about the job search process. It could take three to six months to find the proper fit. Help your cause by dedicating a set amount of time each day to your pursuit, and sticking with it.

success steps for re-entering the workforce

- Awaken your network.
- Do a resumé makeover.
- Consider a career change.
- Contact your former employer.
- Contemplate the work-life balancing act.
- Expect that finding a job will not happen overnight.

 apply it

Conducting Industry Research

GOAL: To conduct research on how an industry has changed

STEP 1: Using a search engine, type in the name of the industry you wish to re-enter (or enter if you are contemplating a career change).

STEP 2: Research job descriptions, industry reports, and other information for changes within the industry, new skills that might be needed, and changes to industry terminology since you left the workforce.

STEP 3: Consider placing the information regarding Conducting Industry Research in your Learning Portfolio.

9

DEMONSTRATING PROFESSIONALISM

As you learned in Chapter 6, demonstrating professionalism during the job search is a critical piece in your ability to gain interviews and successfully secure a job. Once hired into your new position, exhibiting professionalism in your daily work is even more paramount.

Consider the following statistics. The Center for Professional Excellence at York College of Pennsylvania's *2012 Professionalism in the Workplace Study* cites the follow results of their survey of human resources (HR) executives and employee managers on their impressions of recent college graduates when it comes to professionalism:

> ❱ 96% of HR executives/managers believe that professionalism relates to the person, not the job title.

> ❱ 96% of HR executives/managers reported that a job applicant's professionalism affects the likelihood of getting hired.

> ❱ 92.9% of managers stated that an employee's professionalism has an impact on promotion opportunities.

With those staggering statistics, it is little wonder that companies across all industries place an increasing high regard for and value on an employee exhibiting professionalism, no matter what the job title.

ELEMENTS OF PROFESSIONALISM

The *2012 Professionalism in the Workplace Study* participants identified major qualities they feel comprise professionalism. The percentages indicate the importance of each quality.

> ❱ Interpersonal skills: 33.6%. Interpersonal skills include etiquette, being courteous, showing others respect, and behavior that is appropriate for the situation.

> ❱ Appearance: 25.3%. This includes facial piercings other than ears and visible tattoos.

> ❱ Communication skills: 24.9%. This considers both written and oral communication skills.

> ❱ Time management: 20.8%. Time management is further defined as being punctual and using one's time efficiently.

> ❱ Confidence: 20.7%

> ❱ Being ethical: 15.2%

9

> Work ethic: 14.2%

> Knowledgeable: (about the job) 9.3%

Conversely, the respondents ranked the qualities associated with being unprofessional in this manner:

> Appearance: 25.5%

> Lack of dedication: 22.7%

> Sense of entitlement: 22.7%

> Poor work ethic: 22.7%

> Not showing respect: 21.7%

> Poor communication skills: 21.0%

It is no mistake that the correlation between desired and undesired qualities of professionalism is significant. The respondents to the survey wish for certain professional qualities on the job from their employees, but unfortunately witness unprofessional qualities from them all too often.

Finally, in addition to using percentages to indicate the importance of professionalism qualities, the study also used a structured approach where it asked respondents to rate qualities of professionalism in recent college graduates on a scale from 1, not important, to 5, very important. The two highest-ranking qualities were: "displaying a sense of ethics" and "accepting personal responsibility for decisions and actions" (The Center for Professional Excellence at York College of Pennsylvania, 2012).

Exhibiting professionalism while you are on the job should become a manner of daily life. Strive to demonstrate professionalism in everything that you do in your position. Your diligence will pay off as you move forward in your career.

SELF-ASSESSMENT QUESTION

- How would you rate your ability to exhibit professionalism in school, in your job search, in your job?

? CRITICAL THINKING QUESTION

> What steps can you take to improve your ability to demonstrate professionalism?

TEAMWORK

While you are in school, the chances are probably pretty high that you have participated in some sort of team effort for a class, whether it was a team project or presentation. If you have completed an internship, you may have been part of a team as well. In both of these examples, the amount of time that you were on a team was finite, and you will likely never participate in a team activity with those same individuals again.

9

In the work world, you will always be a member of a team, whether formally titled that or not. Teams, and teamwork, are a basic building block of good business and corporate success. Being a "team player" and being able to demonstrate teamwork skills is considered a highly desirable trait by employers. To get the most out of being a successful team member, Gordon (2002) suggests exhibiting the following qualities:

▶ **Enthusiasm and commitment.** A team player shows enthusiasm not only for the job, but the organization as well. A team member shows commitment to the company by embracing the organization's mission, vision, and goals, and seeks to embody them doing daily work.

▶ **Integrity.** Integrity is a cornerstone of an organization's success. If the company does not display integrity with its customers it will not be in business very long. Your ability to display integrity in everything you do in your job will lead to higher potential within the organization. Strive for the highest level of integrity and let your actions as a team member display that level.

▶ **Competency.** Being competent in your job is critical to your team. Highly successful teams are composed of individuals who exhibit competent behaviors and skills at all times.

▶ **Creativity.** Organizations that thrive do so because of their creative thinkers. As a member of your team, let your creativity shine through. Exploring new and creative ways of solving problems means greater success, not only for you, but for your team, and your organization as well.

▶ **Sense of humor.** They say "laughter is the best medicine." And it's true, even in a work situation! Levity can ease tension and allow for refocusing on the topic at hand. And while work is not a joke, making one now and then can be a welcome relief for the entire team.

▶ **Perseverance.** Perseverance is a building block of the team's commitment to achieving its goals. In turn, meeting those goals helps the organization fulfill its vision. Obstacles to achieving team goals should be seen as another opportunity to problem-solve in order to get the job done. High performing teams persevere no matter what stands in front of them.

▶ **Communication.** Our words, whether written or spoken, are the vehicle for self-expression. When you are able to express

9

- In what areas do you feel you need to improve in order to be a successful team member?

▸ What are some pros and cons of seeking out feedback from other team members?

Michael Blann/Lifesize/Getty Images

There are many components to being a successful team, including communication, integrity, and enthusiasm and commitment.

your ideas and feelings to others on the team, you are showing your commitment to not only them, but to your organization as well.

▸ **Questioning ability.** The ability to question is at the heart of a vibrant team. Questioning allows for the creative thought process to flow by seeking out new ways to problem-solve, thus leading to greater results. Successful teams, by nature, question the status quo.

▸ **Reliability and follow-through.** A successful team member is one who says what he means and does what he should in order to get the job done right. A team that has one or more members who cannot be counted on to "pull their weight" will never gain a measure of success. Your words and actions must meet your team's expectation of you as an individual and as a team member.

▸ **Collaboration.** Simply defined, collaboration means working together. Team members who do not collaborate with each other are effectively not a team, but a set of individuals who are assigned the same project. Collaboration fosters trust, creativity, and a desire for success.

success steps for being a successful team member

Successful team members display these qualities:

- Enthusiasm and commitment
- Integrity
- Competency
- Creativity
- Sense of humor
- Perseverance
- Communication
- Questioning ability
- Reliability and follow-through
- Collaboration

MASTERING THE WORK-LIFE BALANCE

The act of balancing work and life is successfully achieved by making sure that all priorities are effectively met—and this is sometimes easier said than done. Meeting priorities effectively means making careful assessments, knowing your resources, and engaging in creative problem solving. Often, balancing outside responsibilities will require making choices based on your priorities at a given time. It also means communicating with your employer and taking responsibility for your decisions.

PRIORITIES IN LIFE

If you have children, you know how illness can interfere with the daily routine. If you don't have children of your own, consider parents, friends, or colleagues who do have children. An ill child presents a significant challenge when the caregiver must be at work or school. Caring for elderly family members or attending to household emergencies can also require immediate attention.

School, gainful employment, family, and home are all *priorities* in your life. At times, certain priorities (such as an ill family member) become more *pressing*. In other words, the more pressing priority requires your focus at a given time and is the priority that receives your immediate attention. Temporarily giving your attention to a more pressing issue does not mean that other aspects of your life are less of a priority—they still are—but they are not the topic of current focus.

Hansen (n.d.) offers the following suggestions for getting your work-life balance in order.

▶ **Ask your employer to modify your current work situation.** If you are a valued employee, you may be in a position to negotiate changes on how you accomplish your job, including flextime, part-time employment, job sharing, or telecommuting, either full time or even a day or two a week. Check with your human resources department or the company's web site to find out policies that govern these types of changes. Approach your employer with a plan and an argument that will convince him that these changes, whether temporary or permanent, will make you an even more productive

9

and valuable employee because you can give your full attention to the job while managing other aspects of your life.

▶ **Switch gears on your career.** Some careers are simply more stressful than others. Now may be a golden opportunity to pursue a career that has been pulling at you for some time. Even if this involves retraining or going back to class, the benefits of not only leaving that stressful job behind but also being able to do what you've wanted to do for some time will be worth it in the long run.

▶ **Seek other employment within your field.** Check your current company to see if there is another position for which you are qualified and that carries less stress with it. Failing that, try a full-blown job search while you are in your current job (but be mindful of not letting on to your current employer that you are doing so), or consider consulting, freelancing, doing temp work, or starting a home-based business (see switch gears on your career, above).

▶ **Slow it down.** This is easier said than done, of course, but it is important that you evaluate where and how your personal time is being spent. Taking time for yourself and getting away from stressors will help both your body and your mind.

▶ **Get organized, get it done.** If you are a disorganized person by nature, you will benefit from trying to organize—and complete—the perpetual to-do list that is life. You will be less stressed if you can prioritize what needs to get done and then check things off as you complete them, whether large or small. Just knowing that things are done will help with your attitude, and that's a stress reliever in and of itself.

▶ **Let others help.** You are not the only one eating the food, creating dirty dishes and clothes, or needing errands to be run. Why should you have all the fun shopping and cooking, doing the laundry and the dishes, and going to the pharmacy and the dry cleaners? Get family members or housemates to pull their weight. It should never be one person's responsibility to run the whole show.

▶ **Leave it for later.** Unless you live with a member of the housecleaning police, it's okay to let things slide once in a while. By not doing some household chores you will being freeing up some time to do something that is more meaningful

> ### success steps for getting your work-life balance in order
>
> - Ask your employer to modify your current work situation.
> - Switch gears on your career.
> - Seek other employment within your field.
> - Slow it down.
> - Get organized, get it done.
> - Let others help.
> - Leave it for later.
> - Seek outside help.

than mopping the kitchen floor. Be mindful, though, of turning this occasional reprieve into a habit. If you house is perpetually dirty that can lead to stress, not to mention a potential health concern.

▶ **Seek outside help.** If you can afford a babysitter, a house-cleaning service, or speaking with a counselor or other professional, take advantage of what these people have to offer.

THE IMPORTANCE OF LIFELONG LEARNING

You are close to your graduation date and are actively pursuing a job in your chosen field. Now that classes will soon be over, you're done with that "learning thing," right? Nothing could be further from the truth! Just because you are no longer attending formal classes does not mean that the learning stops there. *Every* day is an opportunity to learn something new, whether on the job, when you volunteer, when speaking with friends or strangers, when you travel, while you are watching intelligent television, or are reading articles of interest on the Internet or in magazines or newspapers, to name a few.

In our information-centric society of the 21st century, it is virtually impossible not to have access to new and exciting details about the world around us, be it from the past, the present, or speculation about the future. Lifelong learning, while no longer a requirement for

SELF-ASSESSMENT QUESTION

- What are some things you might be able to do at work that will help you with your work-life balance?

CRITICAL THINKING QUESTION

▶ What are some other ways that you can fine-tune your work-life balance?

9

apply it

Lifelong Learning List

GOAL: To identify learning items

STEP 1: In a journal or electronically, write down a list of things you would like to learn moving forward in your life. They can be work-related or just for pleasure.

STEP 2: After you have completed your list, prioritize the items. Then, write down how and when you plan to accomplish the learning.

STEP 3: Revisit your list occasionally. Cross off what you have accomplished, add to or delete items as you see fit, and reprioritize your list.

STEP 4: Consider placing the Lifelong Learning List in your Learning Portfolio.

graduation, unlocks doors where we never thought we held the key. And that's the exciting part—you're not really sure of what is behind any door, or the doors beyond that one.

Lifelong learning can help you in your professional career as well. Employers place value on employees who have the curiosity to seek out new information, whether for the job or not. Continuous learning makes us more interesting people, more well rounded, and more valuable as individuals who can contribute to society in a more meaningful way. That, in turn, can translate into a worker who brings heightening critical thinking and problem-solving skills to the workplace. And that is good for business, no matter what the industry.

You've accomplished a lofty goal by completing your education. Now make another goal for yourself by committing to lifelong learning. You will be glad you did.

CHAPTER SUMMARY

This chapter focused on demonstrating professionalism in the workplace. Emphasis was placed on changes that will likely occur when you first enter the workforce from how your life was while in school. Suggestions were also given for those who are re-entering the workforce after an extended period of time. The elements that comprise professionalism in the workplace were identified as well as behaviors of nonprofessionalism that employers dislike. Teamwork was also a

9

focal point of the chapter, and qualities of what makes an individual a valued team player were discussed. The battle between balancing work life and home life was identified as a daily struggle for many, and suggestions were given as to how to change one's work life in order to achieve a balance. Finally, the importance of lifelong learning was discussed as a valued quality by employers and an important part of one's continued growth as a person.

POINTS TO KEEP IN MIND

In this chapter, several main points were discussed in detail:

- Several areas of your life will change once you enter the workforce, including having less free time than you did in college, the possibility of changing jobs during your career, and the fact that you will not be prepared for all aspects of your new position.

- Suggestions for those re-entering the workforce after an extended time away include reestablishing your network, redoing your resumé to today's standards, the consideration of a career change, and understanding that finding a new job will take some time.

- Elements of professionalism include interpersonal skills, appearance, communication skills, confidence, being ethical, time management, work ethic, and being knowledgeable about the job.

- The two highest-ranking qualities of professionalism as ranked by employers were: displaying a sense of ethics and accepting personal responsibility for decisions and actions.

- Qualities that comprise a good team member include: enthusiasm and commitment, integrity, competency, creativity, sense of humor, perseverance, communication, questioning ability, reliability and follow-through, and collaboration.

- Suggestions for getting your work-life balance in order include: asking your employer to modify your current work situation, switching gears on your career, seeking other employment within your field, slowing down your pace of life, getting organized, letting others help, leaving things for later, and seeking outside help.

- Lifelong learning can help you in your personal life and professional career.

9

CHECK YOUR UNDERSTANDING

 Visit www.cengagebrain.com to see how well you have mastered the material in Chapter 9.

SUGGESTED ITEMS FOR LEARNING PORTFOLIO

▶ Conducting Industry Research. This activity is intended for you to conduct research on what changes have occurred in your industry, what new skills you may need to learn, and what terminology has changed or been added since you left the workforce.

▶ Lifelong Learning List. This activity is designed to get you to identify and prioritize things that you would like to learn going forward in your life.

REFERENCES

Abboud, S. (n.d.). 8 surefire tips for stay-at-home parents to jump back into a career. Quintessential Careers. Retrieved May 22, 2013, from http://www.quintcareers.com/stay-at-home-parents_careers.html

The Center for Professional Excellence at York College of Pennsylvania. (2012). *2012 Professionalism in the Workplace Study.* Retrieved May 22, 2013, from http://www.ycp.edu/media/yorkwebsite/cpe /2012-Professionalism-in-the-Workplace-Study.pdf

Gordon, J. (2002). Top ten qualities of being an outstanding team player. Retrieved May 24, 2013, from http://www.qualitycoaching.com /Articles/team.html

Hansen, R. S., & Hansen, K. (n.d.). Making a successful transition from college to career: time for a reality check. Quintessential Careers. Retrieved May 21, 2013, from http://www.quintcareers.com /college-to-career.html

Hansen, R. S. (n.d.). 10 tips for getting your work/life in balance. Retrieved May 23, 2013, from http://www.quintcareers.com /work-life_balance_tips.html

Walker, D. (n.d.) Baby boomers, beware! Don't let your resume date you! Quintessential Careers. Retrieved May 22, 2013, from http://www .quintcareers.com/baby-boomers_beware.html

9

Index